Photographs by B. A. King

Text by Jonathan Ela

PREFACE BY SIGURD OLSON

The Faces of the Great Lakes

Sierra Club Books   *San Francisco*

We gratefully acknowledge permission to use a selection from
Legends of My People: The Great Ojibway, by Norval Morriseau.
Copyright © 1965. Reprinted by permission of McGraw Hill-Ryerson Limited.
We are also grateful for permission to reprint verses from
"The Wreck of the Edmund Fitzgerald," by Gordon Lightfoot.
Copyright © 1976 by Moose Music Ltd. All rights reserved.

917.7
K

Library of Congress Cataloging in Publication Data
King, B. A.
The faces of the great lakes.
1. Great Lakes region—Description and travel.
I. Ela, Jonathan, 1945–   II. Title.
F551.K55   977'.03   77-7666
ISBN 0-87156-196-4

The Sierra Club, founded in 1892 by John Muir, has devoted itself
to the study and protection of the nation's scenic and ecological resources—
mountains, wetlands, woodlands, wild shores, and rivers. All Club publications
are part of the nonprofit effort the Club carries on as public trust.
There are some 50 chapters coast to coast, in Canada, Hawaii, and Alaska.
Participation is invited in the Club's program to enjoy and preserve wilderness
everywhere. Address: 530 Bush Street, San Francisco, California 94108.

Production supervised by David Charlsen & Others
Printed in the United States of America

To Judy King, and our four children, who suffered
my moods and absences during the preparation
of this book.

B. A. King

To the memory of Walter Ela, whose love for lakes
enriched the lives of the sons he loved even more.

Jonathan Ela

Contents

ACKNOWLEDGMENTS

I am grateful to my parents, whose home in Toronto I used as
a headquarters for almost two years while working on this
book. I always went out to work well-fed and well-rested.

David Suter deserves mention—a splendid black and white
printer—and Ed Swift (my children call him "Mr. Speedo"), a
splendid pilot.

I am also grateful to the people of Eastman Kodak Company. I
am again and again amazed by their dependability and high
standards of quality.

                                                    B. A. King

Rather than recite a long list of names, I would like to thank
collectively two groups of people. First, the helpful myriad
whom I interviewed in offices and libraries, on beaches and
boats, and wherever else I could ensnare a lake lover to my
benefit.

Second, the officers and members of the Sierra Club, who
showed extraordinary patience and encouragement as I labored
far too long away from my professional duties. Two among
this group deserve special mention for their help and understanding: my dear friends and office partners Barbara Halk and
Patricia Record.

Above all, I would like to thank, both retroactively and pro-
spectively, the members of the growing volunteer army in the
United States and Canada who patiently go about the business
of saving our Great Lakes.

                                                    Jonathan Ela

THE GREAT LAKES have been called a river of inland seas. They form a single system of lakes with innumerable tributaries and connecting waterways, a continuous body of water flowing to the ocean. In 1970 some 35 million people lived on both sides of the international border constituted by the lakes—a figure representing one-seventh the population of the United States and one-third that of Canada.

The hard granitic gabbro, greenstone, and hematite formations of the Canadian Shield that hold most of the mineral wealth of Canada and the oil and gas pools found in the ancient escarpment of Silurian dolomites, limestones, and sandstones were formed hundreds of millions of years before the ice ages. The retreating glaciers of that cataclysmic era left a heritage of waters, a tangle of rivers and lakes of which the great five are the most significant to us because of their proximity to civilization. As one studies their configuration on the maps, one begins to surmise the importance of this interwoven complex of waterways which has so influenced our history, and which we, in more recent history, have so influenced.

The legends and lore of the various Indian tribes of the area symbolize the dreams of those peoples who were our precursors there; they provide keys to early human involvement with these waters. The Lakes and the towns and cities beside them often bear names of spiritual significance to the tribes—tokens of their belief in the constant power of the spirit world, and of the past, over the lives of men. We too, in our way, revere the past and carry with us legends from our own history. The opening of the Northwest, largely by the fur traders at first, was a colorful and romantic era, and one from which we retain many such tales. I have followed many of the old traders' routes, like the 3000-mile canoe trip, first made by Etienne Brulé and later by Champlain, leading from Montreal up the St. Lawrence to its confluence with the Ottawa where it swings north, up the height of land to Nipissing, and thence south through the French River to Lake Huron. The Great Lakes were the highway of the explorers and traders, and though many lost their lives in the rapids of the countless rivers they traversed, they were a breed proud of their calling. Daniel Harmon noted in his diary that at one of the wicked portages down through the Dalles of the French, there were forty-one crosses to mark the deaths of canoemen who had lost their lives there. These were the men who carried the trade goods inland, returning with 90-pound bales of fur for the markets of London and Paris.

No longer the old brigades, red-tipped paddles flashing in the sun; no longer the French flag with its golden *fleurs-de-lis* or the bright colors of the Union Jack. All that is far behind, for this is a new age, but we will not forget the voyageurs and their love of a way of life now almost gone. They were the men who pioneered the opening of the Northwest.

The fur trade inevitably brought changes to the Great Lakes. Detroit was established in 1701 as a depot to supply food to the canoe brigades going further into the Northwest. Competing

companies: the XY Company, North West, American Fur, and the Hudson's Bay—the largest of them—were involved in the trade, and there was bloodshed on portages and piracy on the Lakes; the struggle ended only when the various competitors discovered that if they were to survive at all, they must join forces. It was not long before ships began to ply the larger lakes, and some of the old routes were abandoned. Grand Portage began to fade shortly after 1800 and a new post was built at Fort William, which has recently been restored to its former glory.

For both the Indians and the fur traders Manitoulin Island was most significant: their west-bound canoes could proceed across the wild stormy waters of Georgian Bay only in the protected lee of the island. To the Ottawa driven west by the Iroquois, it had been a spiritual home, as it was to the Ojibway who came later for the same reason. And as settlers moved into the Erie, Ontario, and Huron regions, dispossessing the Indians again from their homes, the government decided that Manitoulin was the place for the tribes to relocate—for no one else wanted it. There they stayed in relative peace for some time, until even that sanctuary was taken from them, leaving them only a few relatively small reservations.

I spent my early boyhood at Sister Bay, halfway up Wisconsin's Door Peninsula. There such names as Porte des Mortes ("Death's Door") filled me with fear and delight; as later did the names of Michigan's Upper Peninsula—Dead Man's Point, Escanaba, and Menominee. And another part of my boyhood was spent along the south shore of Lake Superior's Chequamegon Bay. It was there I came to know the famed Apostle Islands, and the Indians of the Red Cliff Reservation.

During the last few decades many reservations of a different sort have come into being on both the Canadian and American side of the border—the many federal, state and provincial parks. Even during the early days of industrial and rural development, when it was considered almost heretical to voice concern for other values, the awareness of the values of preservation did exist. This time saw the first stirrings of the effort to save the 11,000 miles of Great Lakes shoreline from a degradation which even today continues to damage them. Chicago began its effort in 1836, designating its lakefront as "A public ground to remain forever clear and free of buildings or other obstruction whatever." Toronto also had a dream that included a renovated city and its waterfront on Lake Ontario. Minnesota's state parks, for example, now extend from Duluth to the Pigeon River, some 150 miles east, and other preserved lands include Isle Royale National Park, Grand Portage National Monument, the Apostle Islands National Lakeshore, the Indiana Dunes. On the Canadian side many provincial parks and reservations have been established: Lake Superior Provincial Park with its many islands, Pukaskwa National Park, Point Pelee National Park, to name a few.

But still the lakes face serious threats. The swift growth of international shipping from all over the world and the subsequent increased pollution of all waters on which they sail is a continual hazard. Drainage from farms and factories; PCBs; the disruption of food chains with the migration of lampreys, smelt, and alewives into fresh water all pose serious threats which cannot be ignored. The struggles over the Erie and Welland canals, and those bypassing the St. Mary's Rapids continue, but there is hope. Congress has passed the Coastal Zone Management Act; the United States and Canada have established the Great Lakes Quality Agreement, and agencies of the federal, state and county governments, working closely together on pollution control and proper land use, are attempting to find a reasonable approach to the multiplicity of problems facing this diverse area.

Citizens' groups have been formed in both the United States and Canada. Their programs are necessarily lengthy and involved, but they are possible. Innovative planning techniques combined with the purchases of easements and acquisition of lands for parks and reservations provide a start toward reconciling the many contradictory demands made on the Lakes—demands for clean drinking water, fine unpolluted beaches, fishing, transportation, industrial sites and employment, scenic views and breathing space, wilderness and homesites. Despite its problems the Lakes region still represents a treasure of which two nations must be proud.

Sir Wilfrid Laurier, former Prime Minister of Canada, once said, "Almost anywhere on the rough face of the Shield, even fifty miles from Ottawa, it is easy to imagine yourself alone in both space and time."

Once I made a canoe trip with Blair Fraser, a well-known war correspondent and then editor of *McLean's* magazine, and some other Canadian friends from the trading post of Grand Portage. After our trip from Lake Superior to Rainy Lake, Blair's thoughts were very like Laurier's: "This," he said, "is the wilderness empty and lovely. Many places along these lakes and rivers have never been logged and some pines were well rooted when La Vérendrye went through in 1731. Here as nowhere else, men of the 20th century can feel the charm and some of the challenge the makers of Canada knew. What held these people together was not so much love of each other as of the land itself, the vast empty land where for more than three centuries man found himself uniquely at home."

Sigurd Olson

Ely, Minnesota

BEGINNINGS

The River of the Inland Seas

LESS than five thousand years ago, the last of the continental ice sheets—which had covered much of North America off and on for a million years—retreated for the last time back to the Arctic regions from which it had originated. The glaciers left behind them a vastly altered landscape. Among their creations were the Great Lakes, five of the twelve largest bodies of fresh water in the world.

No indication suggests that large lakes existed in the Great Lakes area when the ice age began. In fact, the Lakes appear to have started taking form only during the last of the four distinct periods of glaciation, beginning perhaps eighteen thousand years ago. The lake basins were shaped as the glaciers scraped out troughs. Later, as the glaciers receded northward, the troughs were filled with their meltwater. The moving ice sheets transported and deposited debris, called moraines, over the Great Lakes landscape; in other areas, they smeared a thick layer of sand, gravel, clay, and other material—collectively known as till—over the bedrock.

During the course of twenty thousand years, as the lobes of the glaciers repeatedly advanced and retreated, the Lakes were created, obliterated, and then recreated in altered form. Thus the early versions of the Great Lakes were made and erased again and again. The Great Lakes took the form we know today about thirty-five hundred years ago. In geological terms, the Lakes were sculpted in an astonishingly short time; as features of the earth's crust, they are very young, even in relation to our own human history.

Now, the five great lacustrine legacies of the glacial age—Lake Superior, Lake Michigan, Lake Huron, Lake Erie, and Lake Ontario—are notable features on the map of North America. Less obvious at first glance is the fact that the Lakes are connected, that they form a river of lakes. Runoff from the wild subarctic granite shield of central Canada, the rich prairie topsoils of northern Indiana, the slums and suburbs of Cleveland and Detroit, and the plush resort villages of northern Michigan slowly mixes together in the Lakes and then pours down the St. Lawrence River to the Atlantic Ocean. The Lakes act together as a single system; a disturbance to any one part could have effects everywhere within the system. Yet, for all they hold in common, each lake and each of the connecting channels has its own individual character.

The Great Lakes have no single headwater; rather, a vast network of tiny capillaries eventually flows together to form Lake Nipigon, itself a major lake over sixty miles long and thirty miles wide. From that lake, the waters flow south into the northern extremity of the Great Lakes proper, Nipigon Bay in Lake Superior.

Lake Superior is the wildest of the Lakes; its clear, frigid waters pound against miles of wilderness shoreline. It was named Superior by the seventeenth-century French in the course of their explorations not because of its size, but because it is the most northerly of the five great inland seas. Coincidentally, Lake Superior turned out to be the largest lake as well. In fact, with a total surface area of over thirty thousand square miles, it is by far the largest body of fresh water in the world.

Lake Superior's Canadian north shore is the most rugged and spectacular coast on the Great Lakes. Sheer cliffs plunge abruptly to the water, and the northern tributaries find their ways to the lake through steep and wooded ravines. Waves of crystal-clear water sweep past fantastically shaped offshore boulders and crash against the shore. Much of the shoreline is inaccessible and remains absolutely untouched.

The rock that forms this rugged shoreline is representative of the hard and ancient bedrock called the Pre-cambrian shield. This earliest layer of the earth's crust is composed of hard granite, schists, and other rocks formed more than 500 million years ago by forces of heat and pressure then still active within the restless planet. In some places the shield has been covered by layers of sedimentary rock, but in the upper Great Lakes region the Precambrian rock is covered only lightly with soil or is in some places fully exposed. In this area it comprises a formation called the Canadian or Laurentian Shield, which extends around Lake Superior and lies under the northern edge of Lake Huron as well.

The south shore of Lake Superior is less spectacular than the north, for to the south the shore is lower, and the rugged Precambrian rock is for the most part covered with sedimentary deposits and glacial till. But if this area lacks drama, it does show more diversity. A hint of the northern ruggedness is found on the Keweenaw Peninsula—a spine of Precambrian rock that extends deep into the lake from Michigan—and the Porcupine and Huron mountains also retain their wildness. But Wisconsin's Apostle Island archipelago is characterized by timbered hillsides, beaches, and low bluffs. Michigan's Pictured Rocks are sandstone cliffs stained with a variety of colors; to the east of them, the landscape more resembles the Eurasian Middle East than the American Midwest. The Grand Sable Dunes, perched high above the lake, are a wilderness softer and more subtle than that of the northern forests. These general features of the south shore are varied with innumerable trout streams, rivers tumbling over waterfalls, wild rice bogs, and sandy beaches backed by dense birch forests.

If Lake Superior is the wilderness lake, it is also the lake most affected by resource exploitation. Generations of miners have dug copper and iron ore out of the region and transported it over Lake Superior's waters; before that, the lake served as the base of the northwest fur trade. The northern forests are still being logged, now for the second time, and paper mills are scattered about the shorelines. Here, more than anywhere else in the Great Lakes region, wilderness values clash with the raw facts of resource extraction.

At the southeastern corner of Lake Superior, the wilderness waters funnel through Whitefish Bay and into the St. Mary's River, which eventually empties into Lake Huron. The river is the first

Westward from Whitefish Point stretch for many miles broad beaches of sand and gravel, backed by hills clothed with Norway pines, spruce, hemlock, cedar, and birch. These beaches form extensive fishing-grounds, of which parties had already availed themselves. Everyone knows the superiority of Lake Superior whitefish, in size and flavor, over those of the lower waters.

Bella Hubbard, 1887

of the important connecting channels that stitch the Lakes together into a unified system. A few miles down the river are the twin cities of Sault Ste. Marie in Ontario and Michigan, where man has harnessed the Great Lakes system to serve his own ends. A complicated series of gates and chutes divides the waters and shuttles portions of the St. Mary's River through three power plants, five locks, and a midriver control dam.

The cities of Sault Ste. Marie are also the site of the St. Mary's Rapids. Lock chambers with controllable water levels have been built along the sides of the river, enabling ships to pass by the rapids. A control dam spanning the river permits a degree of control over the water level in Lake Superior and, since the St. Mary's River is a major source of water for the system downstream, the Lower Lakes as well.

After leaving Sault St. Marie, the St. Mary's River flows for about fifty more miles, losing elevation very gradually, before it opens into the northern end of Lake Huron. Huron, the second largest of the Great Lakes, is the least symmetrical. Two large bays bulge out from its sides: on the northeast is Georgian Bay, so large that it is often called "the Sixth Great Lake," while on the other side Saginaw Bay pushes out to the southwest. Lake Huron functions as a bridge within the Great Lakes system; it brings the waters down from the wild north woods to the urbanized southern areas.

The northern and eastern shores of Georgian Bay offer scenery that rivals—some would say surpasses—that of the dramatic coasts of Lake Superior. This region is also Canadian Shield country, perhaps even steeper, wilder, and more rugged than its Lake Superior counterpart. The La Cloche Mountains contain many small inland lakes and slope down to some very wild stretches of Georgian Bay shoreline.

To the southwest, Georgian Bay is separated from Lake Huron proper by a distinctive landform bearing a much quieter and more subtle form of beauty than that of the bay's other shores. The Bruce Peninsula and Manitoulin Island across the channel are limestone spines; they are flatter, more delicate, and less rugged than the wild shield across the bay. They are also more settled; their many small and tidy communities were once based on agriculture but are now increasingly dependent on the urban visitors who come to savor the quiet.

The waters of Georgian Bay are the clearest of any in the Great Lakes. In contrast, the waters of Saginaw Bay are among the most polluted in the system. This bay is shallow and lacks the circulation needed to flush it out. Moreover, it receives the runoff of thousands of square miles of intensively cultivated central Michigan farmland as well as a heavy dose of pollutants from the industrial complexes in Midland, Saginaw, and Bay City along the Saginaw River.

Saginaw Bay's shoreline banks also contrast sharply with those that contain Georgian Bay. Low, composed mostly of compacted sediments rather than rock, they are often lined with cottage development or farm fields. Instead of granitic islands rising from bedrock reefs, marshlands heavily used by waterfowl are found along the lakeshore.

Near the north shore of Lake Huron, the Straits of Mackinac lead west to Lake Michigan, Lake Huron's slightly smaller twin. From a hydrological point of view, Lake Michigan and Lake Huron are two parts of the same lake. The Straits of Mackinac do not constitute a connecting river, such as the St. Mary's, pouring the waters of one lake into another at a lower elevation. Rather, the straits are a deep cut connecting two bodies of water that lie at the same level, in the same way that the Strait of Gibraltar is the passageway between two seas.

Lake Michigan is the lake of fine beaches and great cities. Nearly the entire eastern, or Michgan, coast of the lake consists of sand which forms dunes, banks, ridges, and beaches. The beaches border water that, while not quite as clear as that of Georgian Bay, has the turquoise iridescence usually associated with the Caribbean, a brilliance of hue not found elsewhere on the Lakes. At some places the sands roll back from the water's edge, while in others the dunes perch on top of high banks composed of glacial till.

Chicago and Milwaukee are the most famous of Lake Michigan's cities, but many middle-size metropolitan areas are built along the lakeshore. While the clash between wilderness values and the growth of industrialized society shows on Lake Superior in bold relief, the same conflict occurs on Lake Michigan at a more urbanized, and often more complex, level. Daily the battles are fought and daily the questions are raised. Usually they have to do with priorities. What are the lake's most important resources—drinking water, recreation, potential shipping facilities, wilderness areas, shoreline real estate, cooling water, or freshwater flora and fauna? Lake Michigan provides a text-book demonstration of the critical environmental–industrial conflicts of our day.

At its southern end, Lake Huron—or, as the experts put it, Lake Michigan–Huron—empties into the St. Clair River. A connecting channel less like the St. Mary's River could not be imagined. Instead of coursing through the north woods, the St. Clair flows between the industrial cities of Port Huron and Sarnia, goes on past oil tank farms, and finally sprawls out into a delta of marshy islands as it empties into Lake St. Clair. Like Lake Nipigon, Lake St. Clair might be thought of as a Great Lake in its own right. It is shallow but so broad that from one shore the opposite one cannot be seen. The lake's waters pour out of the basin's south end into the Detroit River, which flows between the heavily built-up areas of Detroit and Windsor, and then into Lake Erie. The connecting channels between Lake Huron and Lake Erie total more than ninety miles in length, but the elevation drop between the two lakes is only eight feet.

Lake Erie is an enigmatic lake. Although it is often described as a dead lake, it has the most productive commercial fishery in the system, and its shores provide the most supportive wildlife habitat. And, despite its reputation as a polluted bog, it is probably the most used, most enjoyed, and, even with its flaws, the most loved lake of the five.

On one dark night on Lac St. Claire
De win' she blo' blo', blo',
An de crew of de wood scow, Julie Plante,
Get scar an' run below.
De win' she blow lak hurricane;
By-n-by she blo' some more;
An' de scow bus' up on Lac St. Claire
T'ree acre from de shore.

Sailors' Song

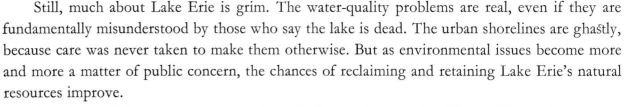

Still, much about Lake Erie is grim. The water-quality problems are real, even if they are fundamentally misunderstood by those who say the lake is dead. The urban shorelines are ghastly, because care was never taken to make them otherwise. But as environmental issues become more and more a matter of public concern, the chances of reclaiming and retaining Lake Erie's natural resources improve.

The Great Lakes waters turn north at Buffalo and enter the Niagara River. They move sluggishly at first but gradually pick up speed until they rush over the rim of Niagara Falls, swirl through a stretch of rapids and whirlpools several miles long, and then, their power exhausted, slowly flow the remaining miles to Lake Ontario. In this thirty-three-mile stretch, the waters make a drop of 325 feet, half of which is accounted for by the vertical drop over the falls. A separate canal with locks a few miles to the west enables ships and boats to pass from Lake Erie into Lake Ontario, avoiding the unnavigable portions of the river and the falls.

Of all the Great Lakes, Lake Ontario, the smallest, has the most subtle features. Visitors will search in vain for the towering bluffs of Lake Superior, the transparent water of Georgian Bay, or the endless beaches of Lake Michigan. On the other hand, the blight conditions usually arising from industrialization and urban development have been held in check surprisingly well, and the water quality, though degraded, has not yielded the fetid algae blooms suffered by Lake Erie. Lake Ontario is the least wild of the five lakes, and its shorelines give the strongest impression of land-scaping; this effect is not achieved through design but rather through a serendipitous mingling of natural forces and human development.

A few miles east of Prince Edward County, which juts into Lake Ontario from the north shore at the lake's eastern end, the Great Lakes narrow down for the last time, and their waters flow through one last constriction into the St. Lawrence River. From Duluth to this point, the waters of the Great Lakes have flowed more than a thousand miles, but they have completed only half their journey, since the open sea is still twelve hundred miles away. Swiftly they flow past the Thousand Islands, the dams and locks of the St. Lawrence Seaway project, and the cities of Montreal and Quebec, until finally they reach tidewater and the Gulf of St. Lawrence.

A demographic perspective on the Great Lakes can be sketched in with a few statistics. In 1970 some 35 million people—one-seventh of the population of the United States and one-third that of Canada—lived in the Great Lakes watershed. Similarly, one-sixth of the national income of the United States, and one-third that of Canada, is generated within the region. Yet of the 11,200 miles of Great Lakes shoreline (including islands) shared by the two nations, over 45 percent, or 5,200 miles, is classified as forested or undeveloped land, and another 15 percent, or 1,700 miles, is categorized as recreational.

These contrasts between population figures and land classification reflect the basic nature of

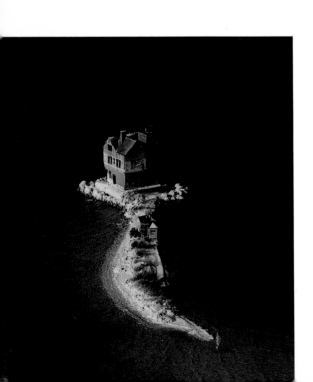

the territory: diversity. The Great Lakes are so vast and varied that the range of experiences they provide their enthusiasts is nearly unlimited.

For some, these waterways are primarily a means of getting from one place to another or transporting goods to far-flung ports. This tradition reaches back to the Indians, who for centuries coursed up and down the Lakes' shores in that most felicitous of inventions, the birchbark canoe. It continued with the arrival on Lake Huron's northern shore in 1610 of the young adventurer Etienne Brulé, and then in the form of wave after wave of explorers, missionaries, and fur traders. And transportation on the Lakes has never been more economically important than it is today, with freighters up to a thousand feet in length carrying raw materials such as iron ore from their sources in the earth to the processing centers and markets of the world.

For many, especially those rooted along the coast, the Lakes offer above all an endless variety of pleasures and relief from the urban environment. Resort areas of many kinds line the Lakes, from the dramatic north shore of Lake Superior to the rocky outcrops of the Thousand Islands, providing seascapes and watery amusements for people far from any ocean. Some avoid well-traveled resorts and seek out their own spots for recreation; the rugged Canadian shoreline of Superior is a favorite with wilderness enthusiasts. And, of course, many users of the Lakes cannot remain contentedly shorebound, but enter into a more intimate relationship with the waters: a family cruises its small sailboat into the entrance of Nipigon Bay; a diver explores a wreck in the clear waters off Lake Huron's Bruce Peninsula; a commercial fisherman leaves from Erie each morning before sunrise to collect his daily harvest of perch and yellow pike.

A connection exists among these various perspectives on the Great Lakes as real as the physical connection that can be traced on a map. If, for instance, a paper mill on Nipigon Bay disgorges a heavy load of wastes into Lake Superior, landowners, sport- and commercial fisherman, and beachcombers and wilderness lovers throughout the system will feel the effects. Shorebound lake dwellers suffer every time industrial development is expressed in a new structure or factory. The Great Lakes together represent not only an interconnected system of waters but also an interdependent system of cultural phenomena.

More than a century ago the Chippewa chief Kichiwiski paddled a canoe from Duluth to Buffalo, and then walked on to Washington to attend a Congressional conference on Indian affairs. When the conference was over he walked back to Buffalo, pushed his canoe out of a screen of willows and paddled the 988 miles back to Duluth. He found the lakes a convenient route to travel. They were a highway, unique in the geography of the earth, linking widely separated regions, ready to carry an Indian on an errand or the bulk commerce of the age of steel.

Walter Havighurst
The Long Ships Passing

The Niagara Escarpment

THE dominant rock formation in the Great Lakes region, the Niagara Escarpment, stretches from Wisconsin to New York. In the Silurian period of the Paleozoic era, some 400 million years ago, a sea filled with small aquatic organisms stretched across the continent's heartland. Year after year, the creatures that inhabited the sea died, sank to the bottom, and decomposed. Their shells remained, however, and ultimately time and pressure petrified this layer of shell into a layer of exceptionally hard rock called dolomite, closely related to limestone.

Other inland oceans swept over the continent, depositing more sediments that eventually turned into layers of rock. When the age of the inland oceans ended, the Silurian dolomite had been pressed far underground. Over the next 180 million years, erosion worked steadily on the overlying rock, and the dolomite was exposed to the elements. But exposure did not occur evenly and all at once. As a result of the constant warping of the earth's crust—localized upliftings and subsidences—the layer of dolomite was more deeply covered by subsequent sedimentary layers in some places than in others.

Silurian dolomite is a much harder rock than that found in the layers that lie above and below it. Therefore erosion occurred more slowly when the dolomite was exposed. Because of its relative hardness, the dolomite layer still protrudes noticeably today, and, because the layer lies at a slant, its exposed edge generally forms either a steep hillside or a cliff. An extensive hillside or cliff of this sort is known as an escarpment. Geologists have named the exposed edge of the Silurian dolomite in the Great Lakes region the Niagara Escarpment.

The Niagara Escarpment surfaces just south of the Door Peninsula on Lake Michigan's west shore and begins a long arc that runs across the tops of Lakes Michigan and Huron, then south along Ontario's Bruce Peninsula and eastward. The horseshoe shape of the arc is very distinct and symmetrical and can be traced easily on a map. As Wisconsin's Door Peninsula, the escarpment forms virtually a mirror image of Ontario's Bruce Peninsula and creates Green Bay between itself and the mainland. Although it is smaller in scale, Green Bay corresponds in shape and location to Georgian Bay, which the escarpment creates in the northeastern portion of Lake Huron.

This great arc embracing Lakes Michigan and Huron resulted from a major land subsidence centered in the state of Michigan that caused all the strata to slope down toward the middle. For that reason, the sharp edge of the layer of Silurian dolomite forming the escarpment faces outward, away from the center of this geological bowl. Therefore, on the Door Peninsula the bluffs look west over Green Bay, while the eastern shore of the peninsula is low and flat; but on the Bruce Peninsula the cliffs face east over Georgian Bay, and the top of the dolomite stratum slopes gently to the west.

In the strait that forms the mouth of Green Bay, the escarpment appears as a series of island outcroppings and reefs; it then dips under the water of Lake Michigan and resurfaces as Michigan's Garden Peninsula. Heading northeast to form the eastern tip of Michigan's Upper Peninsula, the escarpment is at the top of its arc. From here it crops up intermittently to form numerous islands, including Drummond and Cockburn Islands—one on either side of the international boundary. It then rises up as Manitoulin Island, the largest island on the Great Lakes. The physical characteristics of Manitoulin are muted versions of those found on the Bruce Peninsula, further south. The land of the island rolls gently and is dotted with small inland lakes.

The escarpment dips once again into the water of Lake Huron and before surfacing at Tobermory creates small islands and shallow unyielding reefs that have plagued unlucky mariners over the years. The site of despair of those sailors provides a great source of recreation nowadays. This area is the most popular skindiving center on the Great Lakes, and much of the diving activity involves the exploration of old wrecks.

The Bruce Peninsula stretches for more than fifty miles from its tip at Tobermory to its base at Owen Sound. The escarpment's face has an eastward exposure along the peninsula and towers over the clear waters of Georgian Bay. This rim reveals the quintessential Great Lakes shoreline, the stuff that postcards are made of. The shore is marked by a series of deep indentations, each separated from its neighbor by tall headlands. Conifers on these white cliffs dig into any crevice or ledge where erosion may have created a bit of soil.

From the brow of the escarpment forming the peninsula, the flat upper surface of the dolomite layer slopes gently west to Lake Huron. Much of this land was cleared for farming in the nineteenth century, but the soil is thin and extremely rocky. Cleared fields still exist, but a large proportion of the land has been allowed to grow back into second-growth forest, composed largely of maple and other northern hardwoods.

The western shoreline of the Bruce Peninsula is completely different from the Georgian Bay side. The land slides gently into the water with no scenic fanfare. Herons and sandpipers are found on the low beaches and in the marshes and shallow water.

At the southern shore of Georgian Bay, between the cities of Owen Sound and Collingwood, the Niagara Escarpment becomes the Blue Mountains, a heavily wooded, deeply ravined cluster of hills. From here it heads southeast to the mouth of the Niagara Gorge, bisecting the neck of Ontario that separates Lake Huron from the Lower Lakes. As it does so, it forms a stark contrast with the flat farmland through which it cuts. It takes the form of an abrupt, densely wooded three-hundred-foot rise. At the crest is a view of more farmland, flat as a tabletop and stretching as far as the eye can see. The escarpment continues east until it swings south around the end of Lake Ontario, forming the background of the industrial city of Hamilton, and finally finding its most dramatic expression at Niagara Falls.

At the mouth of the Niagara River the flat face of the escarpment, still towering three hundred feet above the flat coastal land at the southwestern shore of Lake Ontario, is slashed by a deep canyon, and through that canyon flow the combined waters of four Great Lakes. Six and a half miles upstream from the mouth of this canyon thunders Niagara Falls, after which the escarpment was named.

The Niagara canyon did not always exist. When the Great Lakes were first being formed, the ice cap still covered this area. The St. Croix, Chicago, Maumee, and Mohawk rivers are all thought to have been outlets from time to time for the earliest versions of Lakes Superior, Michigan, Huron, and Erie. By about 7000 B.C., the ice sheet had retreated far enough for the Niagara River to become firmly established as the outlet for the Lakes. At first, the river carved a shallow path as it left Lake Erie, until it reached the flat, even face of the escarpment. There it tumbled the more than three hundred feet to the plain; no gorge had yet been created, and the falls were nearly twice as high as they are today.

The force of the water was tremendous. Today the natural flow of the Niagara River is over 200,000 cubic feet per second; at times in the past, the glacially swollen Upper Lakes delivered far more than that to the falls. Even Silurian dolomite, hard as it is, cannot resist the buffeting of such an onslaught of water. Bit by bit, slabs of rock fell off the face of the cliff to be pulverized by the force of the water at the base of the falls. Simultaneously, the swirling current at the bottom of the falls ate away the rock beneath it, undercutting the cliff so that more slabs fell off. Niagara Falls is now only 160 feet high, and in the process of consuming itself it has moved six and a half miles back from the escarpment rim. This distance between the falls and the original face of the escarpment is the Niagara gorge. Within it, a series of extremely powerful rapids drops the river the remaining 150 feet. The falls are still moving back at a rate of three feet per year. Ultimately, no Niagara Falls will occur at all; rather, a long Niagara Rapids will drop the 325 feet between Lake Erie and Lake Ontario.

In the meantime, the falls make a spectacular sight. The great curtain of water undergoes a spectral shift as it jumps over the rim, changing from green to white. Sheets of spray rise like a spring shower in reverse, obscuring the base of the falls and dampening the face of the viewer. A thundering boom arises from the gorge; it sounds more like something solid banging against another solid than the sound a liquid should be able to produce.

Even more impressive is the fact that the volume of water in these falls is only a portion of what would be flowing naturally. Two immense hydroelectric facilities have been built to utilize the power of falling water, and these plants divert much of the river away from the falls. By treaty, 100,000 cubic feet per second—half of the average flow of the river—must be left to flow over the falls during daylight hours in the tourist season, while at all other times only 50,000 cubic feet per second must be kept out of the plants' diversion intakes.

Once past the falls, the Niagara Escarpment descends abruptly, and then continues to run eastward. It is last detectable as a range of hills in central New York State running east and west with a steep face to the north.

The Niagara Escarpment is a rocky thread that pulls the whole Great Lakes region together. The technical name for the Great Lakes is the Laurentian Great Lakes, since all are part of an extended St. Lawrence River watershed. But with respect to the elements of scenic continuity that appear throughout the system, they might almost as well be termed the Niagaran Great Lakes.

Indian Lore of the Great Lakes Region

In the recorded history of the Great Lakes many Indian tribes—belonging to three major linguistic families—lived along their shores. The northern and western areas were populated by related tribes speaking various dialects of the Algonkian language: The Ojibway, Ottawa, Potawatami, and Menominee lived in the northern forests, while the Sauk, Fox, Kickapoo, and Miami were Algonkian-speaking tribes of the prairies. To the east were tribes of the Iroquois family. In the region north of Lake Erie and Lake Ontario lived the Neutrals and the Huron; south of those lakes lived the Erie, and, in upper New York State, the famous five nations of the Iroquois—the Seneca, Onondaga, Mohawk, Oneida, and Cayuga. The Sioux linguistic family was represented by only one tribe, the Winnebago, who lived in the Green Bay region.

Each of these tribes had recognized, traditional territories, and many engaged in extensive commerce with each other and with tribes outside of the Great Lakes region. They also conducted ferocious wars, as French explorer Samuel de Champlain, the first European to establish sustained contact with the native populations in the Great Lakes region, quickly discovered. Champlain, who founded a settlement at Quebec in 1608, was instantly pressed into an alliance with the Huron in the conflict they had been waging for years against the Iroquois, a feud that ended in the virtual destruction of the Huron some forty-five years later. One consequence of this war, in which the French sided with by far the weaker party, was that Lake Ontario and Lake Erie—though they were closest to the French outposts on the St. Lawrence—were the last of the Great Lakes to be explored by Europeans, in large part because the threat of the Iroquois made travel on those lakes extremely unsafe.

Probably the longest lasting feud of this kind involved the Ojibway, generally called the Chippewa in the United States, who, at some shrouded date several hundred years ago migrated from their original homeland in eastern Canada to settle in the Lake Superior region. The Ojibway constituted a large tribe and caused a certain amount of territorial upset as they moved west; when they arrived at their new homeland at the west end of Lake Superior, they found the land already occupied by the Sioux. An interminable war was begun. Eventually the Sioux were forced west and had to adapt to the very different environment of the Great Plains. Combat between the two tribes continued intermittently through much of the nineteenth century; not until 1896 did Buffalo Bill Cody arbitrate the settlement that ended the war.

Of all the Indian tribes, the Ojibway have been most closely associated with the Great Lakes. They are still the dominant tribe in the region, living around both sides of Lake Superior as well as along the northern and eastern shores of Lake Huron.

Traditionally, the Ojibway kept small gardens in which they raised such staples as corn and tobacco, but for most of their subsistence, they depended directly on the land and water. Wild rice, which grew abundantly in some of the marshlands, was an important crop. When it was ready to be harvested, the Indians poled their canoes through the sloughs and used sticks to knock the ripened kernels into the bottoms of their boats. The Ojibway who today live in such areas as the Kagagon sloughs of western Lake Superior still harvest wild rice in this way.

Fishing was also important. The Ojibway who lived around the shores of Lake Superior used traps made of poles and basswood fiber netting to catch sturgeon as the fish returned to the Lake from their spawning areas in the tributaries. As the fish blundered into the traps, the Indians killed them with clubs. Ice fishing, which must have required the patience of Job, was also practiced. The fisherman sprawled on his belly on the ice, covering his head and the hole with a blanket to block out light and to permit him to see into the dark water. With one hand he jiggled a lure, and in the other he held in spear in readiness to stab any fish that was attracted.

The Ojibway and the other Great Lakes Indians used the Lakes as a transportation artery. In their birchbark canoes they navigated close to the shorelines on missions of commerce, foraging, and warfare. In the winter they used two other Indian inventions, snowshoes and toboggans, to travel across the snowbound landscape.

And everywhere they went they named things. Four of the Great Lakes have Indian names. Huron and Erie are named after individual tribes. Michigan is from an Algonkian word meaning "big water." Some hold that Ontario is a Huron term meaning "fine lake," although another tradition relates the name to the Iroquois town of Ongniaahra, from which Niagara is also derived.

Some of the Indian names label great places, such as Chicago, which means "wild onion," a plant that used to grow abundantly in the area's marshes. But hundreds of names of small places also are of Indian origin, even if translation obscures the fact. Devils Island, for example, is the outermost island of the Apostle group in Lake Superior. The Ojibway, who lived in the area for centuries, avoided this island, with its water-level caverns that reverberated with the hollow sound of crashing waves, because they believed that an evil *manitou*, a spirit, lived there.

The Ojibway's life was influenced by many manitous, both good and evil. Thunderbird, for

*Off on the lakes the pike-fisher watches and
waits by the hole in the frozen surface,
The stumps stand thick round the clearing, the
squatter strikes deep with his axe.*

Walt Whitman
"Song of Myself"

*Early the red men gave a name to a river,
the place of the skunk,
the river of the wild onion smell,
Shee-caw-go.*

Carl Sandburg
"The Windy City"

example, lived in the hills and made lightning; water beings called Maymaygwaysiwuk moved through the water using stone canoes and stone paddles; and the great water god Misshipeshu dwelled in the bottom of Lake Superior. But the principal figure of Ojibway legend is the demigod Nanabojou, a complex character who in different tales is characterized as ferocious, timid, spiritual, picaresque, admirable, or contemptible. He is well known as Longfellow's Hiawatha, though for some reason the poet chose to change his name to that of a counterpart in Iroquois legend.

Nanabojou created the Indians' land. Ojibway legend contains a deluge that marks the end of the old age and the beginning of the new, and during that flood Nanabojou lived aboard a raft where he was joined by many of his animal friends. After some while, he asked the loon to dive to the bottom and bring him some earth. The loon attempted to do so but failed and surfaced more dead than alive. Nanabojou nursed him back to health and then asked the beaver to carry out the task. The beaver also failed and had to be revived by Nanabojou, as did a number of other animals. Finally, the muskrat managed to reach the bottom and bring Nanabojou a little earth cupped between his paws.

Nanabojou took the dirt in his hands and blew it into the winds. It spread out and became land. After he had created land as far as he could see, he sent the hawk around the world to see if the land was sufficient. The hawk returned in ten days and reported that the waters still covered most of the earth, so Nanabojou sent the muskrat down again and once more blew dirt into the winds. At that point he was satisfied that the Indians had enough land, so he stopped. Today Lake Superior and the other Great Lakes exist, so the legend goes, because Nanabojou stopped blowing dirt into the wind before they were filled up.

Having given the Indians their land, Nanabojou continued to do favors for the Ojibway, giving them, among other things, fire and corn. Fire he obtained by assuming the form of a rabbit and visiting a distant people who were already using it. He went into the village of these people and moved up close to the campfire to get warm and take a nap. When a small flaming stick of the proper size jumped out of the fire, he sprang up, grabbed the still unburned end in his teeth, and scampered off to deliver his prize to the Ojibway.

On another occasion, Nanabojou's grandmother, Nokomis, dreamed that an Indian brave living on the far side of Lake Superior would become an implacable enemy unless defeated by her grandson. So Nanabojou paddled across the lake to a range of mountains where he found the brave and explained that he must vanquish him. The two began to wrestle, and the match went on for a very long time with neither combatant gaining the upper hand. Finally Nanabojou prevailed, and his enemy, whose name was Mandomin, yielded. Upon his surrender, Mandomin offered to become a stalk of green corn so that he would not die uselessly but rather be a source of sustenance forever for Nanabojou's people.

Nanabojou was often the butt of Indians' pranks in spite of all that he had done for them. One example is the story of Nanabojou and the dancing ducks. It seems that one day when Nanabojou saw a number of ducks playing upon the land, he invited them into his wigwam for a party. Since he was their friend, they accepted, and for hours everybody sang, danced, and had a good time. At the end of the evening Nanabojou suggested a game and told all the ducks to dance with their eyes closed. They did so, and Nanabojou danced among them, stooping down to wring their necks one by one. One duck grew suspicious. He opened up his eyes to check and, seeing what was happening, danced over to the door and started to flee. He was almost too late; Nanabojou spotted him and furiously gave chase. Although the duck got away, Nanabojou managed one well-placed kick on his back. "Your back will be flattened forever," screamed Nanabojou, and so it was—that duck became the hell-diver, or grebe.

Nanabojou proceeded to cook his former playmates by building a fire and placing them in the coals with only their legs sticking out. Tired from his dancing, he then fell asleep. While he was napping, a band of Indians passed by. Seeing the ducks in the fire and Nanabojou asleep, they decided to play a trick on him and at the same time feed themselves. They cut the legs off the ducks and carefully replaced them so they stuck out of the fire as they had originally. The ducks themselves they stole to enjoy at their leisure.

Nanabojou woke up from a troubled sleep; he had dreamed that his food was being stolen, so he was greatly relieved to see the ducks' feet still poking out of the fire. When he judged that the ducks were cooked, he pulled them out and was dismayed to discover that he had been tricked.

Most Ojibway legends deal with the natural objects and processes that were important to the culture. They reflect the fact that the Great Lakes Indians lived in harmony with the lands and waters. But this balance between the people and the environment was destroyed with the coming of the Europeans. The Indians themselves changed with respect to the land, becoming couriers, traders, trappers, suppliers, and customers in the fur trade, almost as dependent upon European ways as were the Europeans themselves. Later, as the fur trade waned and their new roles became obsolete, the Indians were either herded together into reserves and reservations or purged. In 1970 the majority of the eastern woodlands Indians in the United States—a grouping which includes those who lived around the Great Lakes—were residents of the state of Oklahoma.

But the Ojibway still devise legends. One, told by Norval Morriseau, an Ojibway from the Lake Nipigon area in Canada, poignantly expresses the confusion wrought by the European invasion of the Indians' land and culture.

> The Great Manitou of all Indian tribes [said to the soul of the recently dead Indian], "As an Indian, by rights you should enter heaven's door here. But you did not practice the faith of your ancestors, you adopted the faith of the white man, Christianity. Go where they have their opening."

Then the soul goes to England, where the white man comes from. Upon arriving at that door where the white man enters, the God of the Christian faiths says, "Although you have practiced the faith of my teachings faithfully, have observed my laws and lived a good life, being an Indian you cannot enter this door. For only the white race goes in here, no Indians. Go back to Canada and go to that door."

Then the soul wanders from place to place, trying the doors of all faiths, and it is not allowed to come in. For the Chinese, Buddhists, or Moslems cannot let the Indian soul in. So what can it do?

I was told that the Indian then goes to the south to join his fellow Indians who have adopted Christian faiths and have forsaken their ancestral beliefs. The place the Indian goes is like a big burned-out forest where crowds of human souls wander.

Finally, with all other hope gone, the Indian's last chance is to reincarnate so that he may live again, this time in that belief in which he would be reborn. Then he is able to enter heaven.

TRANSFORMATIONS

The Fur Trade

NEW FRANCE gained a firm foothold on American soil in 1603, when Samuel de Champlain made his first voyage to Canada on behalf of Henry IV, king of France. Until his death in 1635, Champlain was the guiding influence of the new territory, developing and pursuing four general goals that would remain the basis of French policy in the New World for decades after he was gone from the scene. The first of these goals was exploration of the interior, with a principal view toward finding the long-rumored waterway that would provide a more direct route to the Orient. The second was the building of Christian missions to convert the heathen Indian tribes. The third goal was establishment of trade relations with the Indians in order to acquire furs, and the fourth was the forging of alliances with certain Indian tribes in order to be able to resist pressure from other colonial powers gaining strength in the south. All of these objectives and activities meshed well and guided French policy in varying degrees until the mid-eighteenth century. The French treated their empire purely as a source of spiritual and worldly profit—spiritual in terms of souls and worldly in terms of furs—and in contrast to the English settlements along the Atlantic seaboard, they made little effort to establish permanent communities that would mirror the mother country.

The first of Champlain's minions to transport French goals to the Great Lakes country was the son of a peasant, Etienne Brulé. In 1610 he traveled with a group of Huron Indians to their home along Georgian Bay, and in doing so established the route that would be used by the fur trade for the next two hundred years. Just southwest of Montreal on the St. Lawrence River, the party turned their canoes to the right into the mouth of the Ottawa River; they ascended the Ottawa, then its tributary the Mattawa, and made the long portage out of the St. Lawrence watershed and down into the Lake Nipissing drainage system. After crossing that long lake, they paddled down the French River to its mouth on the northern shore of Lake Huron's Georgian Bay. There Brulé became the first European to see any of the Great Lakes.

Champlain sent other explorers out in Brulé's wake. In 1634 his agent Jean Nicolet passed through the Straits of Mackinac into Lake Michigan, the first European to do so. His more practical mission was to pacify the Winnebago, who were warring with the Huron allies of the French, but Champlain may still have been hoping to find the elusive passage to the Indies. Nicolet arrived at a Winnebago village at the south end of Green Bay, and, according to a legend as charming as it is unlikely, believed he had indeed reached the Far East. It is reported that he donned flowing silk robes, presumably to impress the Ming Dynasty rulers who would turn out to greet him. Finding instead a village of astounded Winnebago, he discharged two pistols into the air, thus establishing himself as a manitou not to be taken lightly.

One of the most significant voyages undertaken on the Great Lakes in the seventeenth century was that of Médard Chouart, Sieur des Groseilliers, and his brother-in-law, Pierre Esprit Radisson, in 1659. In the fall of that year they paddled the length of Lake Superior and spent the winter near the site of Ashland, Wisconsin. The next year they explored the western end of the lake and concluded that access to the territory to the north and northwest would be gained more easily through Hudson Bay. Back in Montreal, Groseilliers found no one interested in backing an expedition to test this theory; he was, in fact, imprisoned for going exploring without official leave. The two had better luck at the court of England's Charles II, where they received the patronage of the king's cousin and adviser, Prince Rupert. In 1670 the Hudson's Bay Company was formed and was granted by royal charter exclusive trading rights to the area that could be served from outposts on the bay.

Many other explorers were sent out through the Lakes by the French governors at Quebec. Some, such as René Robert Cavelier, Sieur de La Salle, were inspired largely by imperial ambitions. La Salle's trips on the Lakes and on the Mississippi River in the 1670s and 1680s were made in the effort to establish a ring of French fortifications that could encircle the English colonists and give permanent preeminence to France throughout the bulk of the continent.

Other explorers were missionaries with a joint interest in scientific discovery and the saving of heathen souls. The most famous of these was Jacques Marquette, who left St. Ignace at the Straits of Mackinac in 1673 and traveled down the Mississippi River as far as the mouth of the Arkansas. Behind these pathfinders came the "organization men." Jesuit missions sprouted up around the Lakes at places like St. Ignace, Sault Ste. Marie, and La Pointe, at the western end of Lake Superior.

The most important of the organizers were the fur traders, the agents of the Montreal-based operations that held charters from the king of France, for the fur trade was the principal reason for the existence of New France. Pelts of all kinds were taken, but by far the most valuable animal was the beaver. Beaver pelts were sorted into many grades. The lowest-grade pelts came from beavers killed in summer; the fur of these skins was notably thinner than the others. The winter kills were classified mainly as to color. But the most prized fur was the lush *castor gras d'hiver*. Such pelts were usually sewn with several others to form a crudely shaped robe and then worn inside out for several months by an Indian trapper. In the process of being worn, the coarse outer hair would fall out, leaving the soft inner fur, which had become even softer from the enrichment of human skin oils.

Regardless of the quality, however, all the pelts ended up in the same place. After they arrived in England, the fur was sliced off the skin, soaked, and placed in a press. Under pressure, the microscopic barbs on the individual hairs firmly intermeshed, and the result was beaver felt. Most of the beaver felt went into the manufacture of hats, those tall, cumbersome hats worn by gentlemen of fashion in England and on the continent.

As soon as the French arrived in the New World, they began to swap goods with Indian tribes for beaver pelts and other hides. Certain tribes were themselves middlemen; they received the French goods and then traveled to more distant regions where they exchanged a portion of their bounty for furs. At first the fur trade was based entirely out of the St. Lawrence area, but as

La Salle unfurled the first sail ever set to the breeze upon Lake Erie, and upon the *Griffin*, a schooner of forty-five tons burden, made the voyage to Lake Huron. In 1682 he reached the Mississippi, descended to its mouth, and there solemnly proclaimed possession of the vast valley in the name of his king.

*1812 History of
Sandusky County, Ohio*

The reader may first turn his eyes to the Mission of Sainte Marie du Sault, three leagues below the mouth of Lake Superior. He will find it situated on the banks of the river by which this great Lake discharges its waters, at the place called the Sault, very advantageous in which to perform Apostolic functions, since it is the great resort of most of the Savages of these regions, and lies in the almost universal route of all who go down to the French settlements.

Claude Dablon
Jesuit Relations for 1671–2

the more accessible populations of beaver were exterminated while the demand continued to increase, the trade relentlessly worked its way north and west.

In 1679 a permanent post was established at Kaministikwia, on the western shore of Lake Superior, in order to encourage trade in the backcountry, and by the end of the century, Mackinac was the center of the trade. In the 1740s and 1750s, the French built posts on Rainy Lake, Lake of the Woods, Lake Winnipeg, and beyond.

Then suddenly the whole enterprise terminated. On September 13, 1759, the long colonial struggle between France and England took an irrevocable turn when the army of General James Wolfe defeated that of General Louis Joseph de Montcalm on the Plains of Abraham outside the city of Quebec. Under the Treaty of Paris of 1763, France yielded all of her North American possessions, with the exception of a few Caribbean islands, to Britain and Spain.

The French legacy around the Great Lakes was nothing but an expanse of undeveloped wilderness, or so it must have seemed at first sight to the inheriting Britishers. The interior west of Montreal held few settlements, and even where a permanent town had been established, it was generally designed around the fur trade. Detroit, for example, was settled in 1701, in large part to supply grain to Mackinac and the other centers of the fur trade.

Aside from its missionary efforts, France's interest in the New World had been limited largely to the accumulation of hard, cold cash from the Parisian hat industry, which accumulation in turn depended on *Castor canadensis*, the beaver. Settling the area—clearing the forests, establishing agricultural settlements, encouraging immigration—was inimical to the trade in beaver pelts. When France relinquished her rights to the Great Lakes region in 1763, the land looked almost exactly as it had when Etienne Brulé first traveled to Georgian Bay 153 years earlier.

The French had had a few major impacts, however. Most significant, the Indian culture had changed. A copper kettle was more portable and efficient than a bowl carved from the hard trunk of a tree; firearms could bring down game more easily than a bow and arrow. European-made trinkets graced the body with more dash and color than ornaments crafted from local resources; wool blankets offered advantages over fur rugs; and firewater eased the rigors of wilderness life more quickly than the shamans could. By 1763 the Indians were no longer independent. They had become careerists—trappers and traders for the French. And they no longer simply took what they needed, confident that the good land would support them indefinitely. Instead they stripped the land to fulfill the needs of the French, which far exceeded the original needs of the Indians. In doing so they were able to supply themselves with European products, which entered their lives as novelties but quickly became necessities.

This self-feeding circle revolving around the fur trade led to the greatest physical change in the Great Lakes region during the French period. The Lakes may have looked the same along the

Demande une femme à prendre,
Demande une femme à prendre,

Ne prenez pas une noire,
Car elles aiment trop à boire,
Ne prenez pas une rousse,
Car elles sont trop jalouses.

French-Canadian
Boatmen's Song

shorelines, but in the surrounding wilderness the beaver had been largely eradicated. By the mid-eighteenth century, the Great Lakes were no longer a vast hunting region for furs but rather a watery corridor leading ultimately to the centers of fur activity in the far northwest.

Even before the treaty ending the war was executed, ambitious English-speaking entrepreneurs moved into Montreal to fill the vacuum in the fur trade. They entered the field with gusto, and for two decades competition among British traders was heavy. With the exception of a relatively small number of new faces at the top, the British-dominated fur trade during this period was identical to that during the later years of the French period. The guides and voyageurs were still French Canadians, as they were to be in the nineteenth century as well. Most of the posts were traditional French sites that were simply taken over by the new firms and rebuilt as necessary. The canoes, the routes, the Indians with whom the traders dealt, and all the other techniques and trappings of the trade were the same as they had been for years. The political shift ratified by the signing of the treaty in 1763 made only minor differences in the fur trade's operation: the trade goods were British instead of French, the pelts went to London instead of Paris, and a different set of merchants garnered the profits.

In the late 1770s, a young Scottish-born trader named Simon McTavish emerged as a key leader of the industry. In 1783 he helped found the North West Company, which squeezed out and absorbed the weaker operators one by one, and in 1787 he established his own firm, McTavish, Frobisher and Company, as North West's Montreal agents. When the parent firm, under the leadership of MacTavish's nephew, William McGillivray, absorbed Alexander Mackenzie's XY Company in 1804, the task of putting together an effective monopoly had been completed.

The original site of the company's field operations was the old French post at Grand Portage on the northeast shore of Lake Superior just south of the Pigeon River, which formed the route into the northern wilderness. In 1796, Jay's Treaty established the Pigeon River as the international boundary, and Grand Portage lay on the American side. The company was unable to overcome the political problems that the boundary created, so in 1803 Grand Portage was abandoned, and the North West Company's operations moved up the shore to the new Fort William at the mouth of the Kaministikwia River.

The Montreal canoes used by the voyageurs had a remarkable carrying capacity. The following inventory, compiled by a late-eighteenth-century fur trader, lists the contents of one canoe bound from Montreal to Mackinac:

16 bales of dry goods
12 kegs of rum
2 kegs of wine
4 kegs of pork and beef

ART. III. It is agreed that it shall at all times be free to his Majesty's subjects, and to the citizens of the United States, and also to the Indians dwelling on either side of the said boundary line, freely to pass and repass by land or inland navigation, into the respective territories and countries of the two parties, on the continent of America (the country within the limits of the Hudson's Bay Company only excepted) and to navigate all the lakes, rivers and waters thereof....

Jay Treaty
November 19, 1794

2 kegs of grease
1 keg of butter
3 cases of iron work
1 case of guns
6 kegs of gunpowder
4 bags of shot and ball
4 bags of flour
4 rolls of Brazil tobacco
4 bales of tobacco

Besides these items, which were bound for the trading post, the canoe had to carry nearly 1,500 pounds of food and equipment for the month-long journey itself, personal belongings of the voyageurs, and such necessities as paddles and extra birch bark for repairs. When the weight of the men themselves was added—listed as nine men at 140 pounds per man—the total load of the canoe came to 8,250 pounds, not including the weight of the canoe itself.

The annual cycle of activity of the company was to remain the same for the first two and a half decades of the nineteenth century. Each May a fleet of dozens of heavily laden canoes pushed off from the shore of Montreal to start the six-week-long journey to Fort William, following the same route to Georgian Bay that had been pioneered by Etienne Brulé. Paddling hour after hour—often against the current—and portaging the thousands of pounds of merchandise and supplies dozens of times was backbreaking work. Toward the end of the journey came the worst part: the hazardous trip across Lake Superior. Ultimately the North West Company built a small sailboat on the lake to carry some of the load and lighten the canoes a bit, but working the canoes slowly along the red-rock northern rim of the lake was still hard labor. When they finally reached the mouth of the Kaministikwia, the members of the fleet indulged themselves in drunken celebration.

Meanwhile, a similar procession was under way in the west. Throughout the seemingly endless winter of the Canadian northwest, Indian tribes had been trapping furs: fox, moose, marten, buffalo, muskrat, and, most important, beaver. By the time the ice was breaking up at each of the North West Company's one hundred trading posts—scattered from Lake Superior through the Athabasca country to Great Slave Lake—the season's furs had been bought and packed into ninety-pound bales. In late spring the traders in their *canots du nord*—slightly smaller than the Montreal canoes—started working their way down a hundred different capillaries through the wilderness, converging on Lake Winnipeg, Lake of the Woods, Rainy Lake, and, ultimately, the Kaministikwia River and Fort William.

For two weeks in July, Fort William went wild as the Montrealers and the winterers mingled together at the annual rendezvous. The permanent population of the fort was never much more

I now learned, that M. Leduc, in the earlier part of his life, had been engaged in the fur-trade, with the Indians of Michilimackinac and Lake Superior. He informed me of his acquaintance with the Indian languages, and his knowledge of furs; and gave me to understand, that Michilimackinac was richer, in this commodity, than any other part of the world. He added, that the Indians were a peaceable race of men, and that an European might travel, from one side of the continent to the other, without experiencing insult. . . .

The inland navigation, from Montreal to Michilimackinac, may be performed, either by the way of Lakes, Ontario and Erie, or by the river Des Outaouais, Lake Nipisingue and the river Des Francais; for, as well by one as the other of these routes, we are carried to Lake Huron. The second is the shortest, and that which is usually pursued by the canoes, employed in the Indian trade.

Alexander Henry, Esq., 1809

than forty people, but during the rendezvous some two thousand company employees drank, fought, and generally raised hell along the shore of Lake Superior. During this period in July, the partners met in the Council House to decide the affairs of the company. When the rendezvous was over, the voyageurs and traders exchanged cargoes and departed. The men of the north took the newly arrived trade goods back up to their far-flung posts in order to secure more furs from the Indians during the next winter, while the furs themselves were sent down to Montreal, and eventually to England.

But, by the rendezvous of 1816, the North West Company was in deep trouble. In part this trouble was due to the nature of competition. To the south, John Jacob Astor's American Fur Company had emerged and was restricting the trapping grounds available to the North West Company. And in Canada the North West Company's traditional rival, the Hudson's Bay Company, was asserting a strong advantage. Hudson's Bay Company was already over a century old at the time McTavish established the North West Company.

As the more accessible populations of fur-bearing animals were depleted and the North West Company had to extend its operations farther and farther westward for profits, the company became more and more expensive to run. A glance at a map of Canada will confirm the advantage held by the Hudson's Bay Company. The broad rivers leading into Hudson Bay, and thus to the oceanbound sailing ships, provided much more direct, and hence much cheaper, routes than the canoe route to Montreal via Fort William and the Great Lakes. Radisson and Groseilliers, who established the Hudson's Bay Company on this premise in 1670, had been correct.

But the Hudson's Bay Company was embarking on an enterprise that posed an even more direct threat to the North West Company. Thomas Douglas, the fifth Earl of Selkirk, and his family controlled a substantial portion of the Hudson's Bay Company, and Selkirk was determined to use the company as a vehicle for colonizing the North American interior. In 1811 he set out to develop a colony in the Red River valley, in parts of what are today Manitoba, North Dakota, and Minnesota.

Settlement and fur trading were still considered to be totally incompatible, just as they had been during the French period. Selkirk's Red River Colony was viewed by the North West Company, and by the independent traders who relied upon it, as an intolerable threat to its interests, usurping trapping grounds that had been considered part of the Montrealers' traditional jurisdiction.

Matters came to a head in the summer of 1816. A group of halfbreed buffalo hunters attacked the Red River Colony and killed twenty-one settlers in the battle of Seven Oaks, the site of which today lies in downtown Winnipeg. Convinced that the North West Company had incited the assassins, Selkirk vowed to retaliate. In mid-August, a few weeks after the company's annual rendezvous had dispersed, he arrived at Fort William armed with legal warrants and mercenary

Afterwardes we entered into a straight which had 10 leagues in length, full of islands, where we wanted not fish. We came after to a rapid that makes the separation of the lake of the hurrons, that we calle Superior, or Upper. . . . . This rapid was formerly the dwelling of those with whome wee weare. . . . Wee made cottages att our advantages, and found the truth of what those men had often [said], that if once we could come to that place we should make good cheare of a fish they call Assickmack, which signifieth a white fish. The beare, the castors [beavers], and the Orinack [moose] shewed themselves often, but to their cost; indeed it was to us like a terrestriall paradise.

Account by Pierre Esprit Radisson

soldiers. He seized the fort and arrested the half-dozen North West Company partners who were still present, including William McGillivray. All but one of the partners were escorted under armed guard to Montreal, where commenced, in the fall of 1816, a series of legal proceedings and public recriminations that was to dominate the interests of both companies for the next five years. Fuel was added to the furor when McGillivray and his colleagues learned that the partner who had remained at Fort William, Daniel Mackenzie, who had no authorization to make such a deal, had been induced by an artful combination of imprisonment and alcohol to sell the entire contents of the fort to Selkirk.

The North West Company regained possession of Fort William in 1817, and the death of Selkirk in 1820 eased relations between the two firms to some degree. But the North West Company was fundamentally in a hopeless position, with only one way out. In 1821 the North West partners took their only option, and the two great companies merged. The North West Company thereby passed into history, since the name of the Hudson's Bay Company was retained for the consolidated operation.

The last rendezvous at Fort William took place in 1821. Although the fort continued to function for another sixty years as a minor outpost, the consolidated firm immediately shifted its major operations to Hudson Bay. Thus ended the Great Lakes fur trade. By 1816, the year of the last carefree rendezvous at Fort William, the beginnings of cities were already established on the Lower Lakes and sailing ships were already carrying settlers farther afield into the winderness. A few years later the construction of the Erie and Welland canals accelerated that process enormously. And by midcentury European civilization had gained toeholds along every stretch of Great Lakes shoreline. Steamships bearing settlers, timber, limestone, and the necessities for permanent living replaced the fleets of canoes with their furs and trading goods.

The Experiment on Manitoulin Island

MANITOULIN ISLAND, in Lake Huron, is the largest island on the Great Lakes. It is the northernmost of two large segments of the Niagara Escarpment that separate Georgian Bay and the North Channel from Lake Huron proper. By Ottawa Indian tradition, the island is a sacred place, home of the Kitchi *manitou*, the most powerful of the spirits in the pantheon of the Algonkian Indians. The *manitou* was said to live in a grotto at the head of Manitowaning Bay, with his people living in scattered villages around the island. The original Indian name for Manitoulin was Odawa-miniss, "Isle of the Ottawas."

In the mid-seventeenth century, the Ottawa fled from the island, driven off by the Iroquois, whose armies swept north from their New York State homeland and conquered the Huron and other tribes living on the neck of land between Georgian Bay and the Lower Lakes. Under this pressure by the Iroquois, the Ottawa moved north and west; for more than a hundred years after that, Manitoulin Island appears to have been almost completely uninhabited. Gradually it was resettled by bands of Ojibway, but even by the beginning of the nineteenth century it was very sparsely settled. In the nineteenth century the island again became an Indian population center, but under very different circumstances than ever before.

In the days of the Great Lakes fur trade, the white entrepreneurs relied heavily on local Indian tribes, but by the early nineteenth century the symbiosis that had existed between the natives and the colonialists was coming to an end. The fur-bearing animal populations of the region had by then been decimated, and the Lakes had become simply a well-known corridor for reaching trapping grounds much farther west. With the consolidation of British power in Canada and the indisputable existence of a separate nation to the south, the possibility of a conflict among European powers became remote, and maintaining alliances with Indian tribes was no longer critical. In fact, the British not only ceased to value such alliances, but also they began to view the Indian populations as hindrances to settlement and expansion. For the Indians' part, the benefits they had received from the whites—better weapons, portable kettles, ready-made clothing, and the like—were quickly outweighed by British encroachment onto their lands and by the hostility and contempt with which they were ever more frequently treated.

The British grew increasingly determined to move the Indians out, and they drew up treaty after treaty to do so. In Upper Canada, separate treaties—in 1798, 1815, 1818, 1836, and 1851—nullified Indian ownership of nearly all the land lying south and west of Lakes Ontario and Erie and north and west of Lake Huron and Georgian Bay. The government then surveyed the land and sold it to settlers or speculators. The trees were logged and shipped away for use in building cities, and farms and communities sprang up in the former tribal lands.

Needless to say, tension between the natives and colonialists increased. Even if the Indians had been willing to vacate their land simply because they had signed a treaty, the terms of which were frequently unclear, nowhere remained for them to go which the British had not already claimed for themselves. In 1836, when it became evident that the two cultures could not coexist on land that both populations considered their own, the government decided that the Indians must be isolated. The area chosen for the Indians of Upper Canada by Sir Francis Bond Head, governor of Upper Canada, was Manitoulin Island and its neighboring islands in the North Channel of Lake Huron.

This resettlement scheme had a number of advantages from the government's point of view. First, and most important, the Indians of Upper Canada would be concentrated in an isolated location where they would not interfere with the agricultural development of their former lands, and

Many moons ago, when the Indian people owned all the land from the Manitoulin to the Blue Mountains, tribes lived within a few arrows' flight of one another. There were many wars. . . . Toward the end of the eighteenth century, the son of a powerful tribal chief fell in love with the daughter of another chief, and ran away with her.

The lovers travelled by canoe. Soon the maiden's father assembled his warriors and set off after them . . . The young lover remembered the Island of the Caves and hurried there to hide his sweetheart . . . But the maiden's father had also thought of this . . . The young brave was killed, and the maiden died of a broken heart.

Since that time, Indians have called the island the Island of the Flower Pots, and they claim that the two flower-pot formations are the stone spirits of the young Indian lovers. To them that island is a forbidden place, and they will not set foot on its shore.

Melba Croft
*Tall Tales and Collections
of the Georgian Bay*

where they would not be abused and corrupted by the new frontier communities. Second, Manitoulin Island was thought to offer the Indians the opportunity either to pursue their traditional styles of living, based largely on hunting and fishing, or to take up agriculture and become modern themselves. Third, concentrating the Indians in one area would advance efforts at "civilizing" them through government- and church-sponsored schools and missions.

Manitoulin was also deemed an ideal location for the annual gift ceremonies. The treaties signed with the Indian tribes provided that the natives would receive annual compensation in exchange for relinquishing their lands, and each summer the tribes arrived at a rendezvous point to receive their payments in goods and merchandise. Prior to relocation, these ceremonies, at which thousands of Indians gathered, were held at Amherstburg on the Detroit River, and at Drummond and St. Joseph Islands at the mouth of the St. Mary's River. Both areas abutted the international boundary, and the ceremonies were swamped with Indians who crossed from the United States insisting on compensation, though they had not been parties to any of the treaties and did not come under Canadian jurisdiction. The government hoped that Manitoulin Island would prove to be sufficiently distant from the border to discourage these transient panhandlers.

In 1836 the government was attempting to wheedle the Bruce Peninsula away from the Sauking Indians. In exchange, Governor Head offered the opening of Manitoulin Island for all Upper Canadian Indians. At the same time he had to negotiate a treaty with the Ottawa and Ojibway residents of Manitoulin by which those tribes would permit the Sauk and others to settle on their lands. This document, written in a tone of paternalistic cajolery, is a good example of the style used by the government when addressing the populations it was shuffling around:

My Children:

Seventy snow seasons have now passed away since we met in Council at the crooked place, at which time and place your Great Father, the King, and the Indians of North America tied their hands together by the wampum of friendship.

Since that period various circumstances have occurred to separate from your Great Father many of his red children, and as an unavoidable increase of white population, as well as the progress of cultivation, have had the natural effect of impoverishing your hunting grounds, it has become necessary that new arrangements should be entered into for the purpose of protecting you from the encroachment of the whites.

In all parts of the world farmers seek for uncultivated lands as eagerly as you, my red children, hunt in your forest for game. If you would cultivate your land it would then be considered your own property, in the same way as your dogs are considered among yourselves to belong to those who have reared them; but uncultivated land is like wild animals and your Great Father, who has hitherto protected you, has now great difficulty in securing it for you from the whites, who are hunting to cultivate it.

The canoe being ready, I went to the upper end of the portage, and we launched into the river. It was a small fishing canoe about ten feet long, quite new, and light and elegant and buoyant as a bird on the waters. I reclined on a mat at the bottom, Indian fashion, (there are no seats in a genuine Indian canoe); in a minute we were within the verge of the rapids, and down we went with a whirl and a splash!—the white surge leaping around me. . . . The Indian with astonishing dexterity kept the head of the canoe to the breakers, and somehow or other we danced through them.

Anna Jameson, 1839

Under these circumstances, I have been obliged to consider what is best to be done for the red children of the forest, and I now tell you my thoughts.

It appears that these islands on which we are now assembled in Council are, as well as all those on the north shore of Lake Huron, alike claimed by the English, the Ottawas and the Chippewas.

I consider that from their facilities and from their being surrounded by innumerable fishing islands, they might be made a most desirable place of residence for many Indians who wish to be civilized, as well as to be totally separated from the whites; and I now tell you that your Great Father will withdraw his claim to these islands and allow them to be applied for that purpose.

Are you, therefore, the Ottawas and Chippewas, willing to relinquish your respective claims to these islands and make them the property (under your Great Father's control) of all Indians whom he shall allow to reside on them: if so, affix your marks to this my proposal.

All the necessary marks were duly affixed, and the Manitoulin experiment proceeded. The Indians were to be encouraged, though not coerced, to move to this land, thought to be in its abundance and fertility a perfect place for the Indians to become civilized. Conveniently enough for the government's purposes, because of its isolation, harsh climate, and thin stony soils, it was also considered uninhabitable by Europeans.

In keeping with its determination to teach the Indians culture and manners, the government proposed to set up an "Establishment," or mission, on the island. In October, 1838, a *bateau*—a small flat-bottomed boat used most frequently by the Europeans on Canadian waterways—left the southern end of Georgian Bay for Manitoulin, some two hundred miles away. It carried thirty-four people—a superintendent from the Indian Department, an Anglican missionary, a doctor, various artisans and laborers, and all the members of their families, including twelve young children—in short, the Establishment of Manitoulin Island. The party was traveling very late in the season and had a hard journey, but, finally, after three miserable weeks spent creeping up the inside passage through the Thirty Thousand Islands, it arrived at Manitowaning. The Establishment's first sight upon disembarking was the burning to the ground of one of the houses that had been built for them. That omen set the tone for the difficult winter that followed. A supply ship was to have provided the group with its winter necessities, but it encountered unseasonably early ice and had to turn back before reaching the island.

The party subsisted through the winter on a daily ration of half a slice of bread per person, some potatoes that fortunately had been harvested the previous summer and left for them, whatever fish and game could be captured with the help of the Indians, and a plentiful supply of maple sugar. Two of the children died early in the winter.

Once the hard winter passed, more houses were built, along with shops for the artisans and a combination warehouse and church, and the Indian school was established. Here the Indians were taught standard school subjects as well as agriculture, carpentry, blacksmithing, and other crafts. They were read to from the Bible and from *Pilgrim's Progress.*

In the early years, the Establishment seemed to be succeeding in its mission to educate the Indians on the island. By 1842 the Indian population at the Manitowaning Establishment had reached about two hundred, though a larger number, about 350, had settled at a rival Roman Catholic mission at Wikwemikong. Many Indian groups came voluntarily to the Establishment and then gradually drifted off to other parts of the island where they lived in traditional fashion. The Indian population swelled each summer when more than five thousand Indians arrived for the annual gift ceremonies. Many of those who arrived were, after all, Indians from the United States; they proved to be far more enterprising than the authorities had expected and were willing to travel great distances for the occasion.

The accounts of the Manitoulin settlement were enthusiastic. Residents noted that their missionary efforts were making progress, and visiting clerics were delighted at the enthusiasm shown by the converts, regretting only that such a large proportion of the flock had been ensnared by the Papists at Wikwemikong. The Establishment members were convinced that their program was humane and progressive and that it was succeeding.

But by 1860 the government decided that the Manitoulin experiment had failed. For some years the population had been static, with new Indian settlers being counterbalanced by those who left to return to their original homes. Moreover, most of the new arrivals were Ojibway from the wilderness around Lake Superior who felt comfortable in the harsh climate and rugged environment of Manitoulin, while those departing were Indians from Upper Canada, for whom the reserve had been intended but who were unable to adjust to the hostile conditions on the island. The government was vexed: The point was not to bring new Indians in from afar but to isolate those who were competing with settlement.

Undoubtedly an additional element contributed to the government's disenchantment: By 1860 the richer and more accessible areas of Upper Canada had been settled, and Manitoulin could no longer be considered a superfluous and barren territory. British proponents of settlement questioned whether the land on Manitoulin should be used inefficiently to support a few hundred Indians, when it could be extensively cultivated to provide food and livelihood for many times that number of whites. In his treaty twenty-five years earlier, Governor Head had stated, "In all parts of the world farmers seek for uncultivated lands as eagerly as you, my red children, hunt in your forest for game." Now the European settlers were becoming hard-pressed for the same commodity.

In 1862 the government sent a team of negotiators to conclude a new treaty with the Manitoulin

Indians. Those living at Wikwemikong at the eastern end of the island stoutly refused to sign a treaty giving away their land, while the others scattered around the island were more tractable. As a result, the Manitoulin Island Unceded Indian Reserve, with an area of about 125,000 acres, was established for the Wikwemikong Indians. Today it is still the largest Indian reserve or reservation along the Great Lakes. The other Indians signed the treaty. In exchange they received homesteads of one hundred acres per family, the proviso being that the homesteads were to be tightly grouped together on contiguous lands. In addition, the Indians were to receive the bulk of the revenues resulting from the sale of Manitoulin lands to settlers. The legacy of this agreement is five small Indian reserves, totaling a little over 20,000 acres.

Thus in the 1860s the settlement of Manitoulin Island entered a new phase. Originally the island had been the spiritual home for a powerful nation of Indians; later it was at least intended as the temporal home for numerous Indian populations faced with dislocation as a result of white settlement. Now it was to be the white man's country, an agricultural paradise for Canada's landless immigrants. The island was surveyed, and the more than 80 percent of the land that the Indians signed away was sold off to settlers. The land was cleared of timber, the fields were cleared of rocks and stumps, and farming became the main concern. Towns such as Gore Bay and Little Current sprang up on the edges of the North Channel to receive the ships that were the sole lifelines to civilization—except for the hazardous crossing of the winter ice—until the Algoma Eastern Railway island-hopped its way to Manitoulin in 1914.

But the northern reaches of the Niagara Escarpment are difficult areas for farming. The soil is thin and rocky, the northern winters are harsh, the growing season is short, and markets are a long distance away. As was the case with many other areas around the Upper Lakes, after the staggering amounts of labor needed to clear the land were performed, the land itself proved ill-adapted for farming. Today, as a result, agricultural activity is another phase in the island's past. Second-growth forest is the predominant ground cover now; most of the fields that remain are overgrown, and abandoned farmsteads are to be found all over the island. And Manitoulin's chief industry today is tourism.

The Creation of Sandusky

IN 1817, the year following Lord Selkirk's invasion of Fort William, Sandusky, Ohio, was platted and opened for settlement. The history of Sandusky is in many respects representative of that of many small cities on both sides of the Lakes, although it takes certain twists and turns of its own. It begins in 1662, when King Charles II granted the young John Winthrop a charter defining and making permanent the boundaries of the recently consolidated colony of Connecticut. Winthrop made a good bargain, for after defining the metes and bounds of the northern and southern boundary lines of what is today the state of Connecticut, the charter extended the colony west the breadth of the continent to what was commonly called the South Sea.

Had these boundaries been maintained, the state of Connecticut would today be some seventy miles from north to south and three thousand miles wide, a situation that no doubt would have presented what government employees like to call "administrative problems." But the fickle English monarch quickly destroyed this intriguing possibility by issuing conflicting charters to the colonies of New York and Pennsylvania. The three colonies squabbled over the western lands for decades, and Connecticut finally lost her Pennsylvania lands in a commission ruling in 1782. By this ruling, however, she still maintained ownership of and jurisdiction over a strip of land running from the western boundary of Pennsylvania to the South Sea, lying between the parallels of latitude 41° and 42°2′ north. A series of compromises further trimmed the glory of Connecticut until she ceded all her lands except a strip between the forty-first parallel and Lake Erie, running west for a hundred and twenty miles from the Pennsylvania border. This territory of 3.6 million acres was known as the Connecticut Western Reserve. Physically it was owned by the state of Connecticut, but it lay under the civil jurisdiction of the territory, later the state, of Ohio.

Connecticut's first decision on how to dispose of its western empire resulted from an incident that took place during the Revolutionary War. On July 5, 1779, the English fleet bombarded and set fire to the city of New Haven and then went on to cause great damage to eight other coastal cities. For thirteen years these cities and their inhabitants petitioned the state to grant financial relief for the suffering and damages incurred during the British raid, and finally in 1792 the Connecticut General Assembly decided to separate out the western half-million acres of the Western Reserve and use the proceeds of the sale of this tract to aid the communities. Thereafter the tract was known as the Firelands, in commemoration of the Connecticut towns that burned during the Revolutionary War.

Working out the details of disposal took another fifteen or so years. The land had to be surveyed, Indian claims extinguished, a proprietary company of representatives of the affected coastal towns established, and equitable means of disposal and disbursement arranged. By 1810 the Sufferers Land Company had received and distributed the Firelands, and private associations were already speculating and arranging for the resale of tracts and lots to private citizens.

The disposal of the public lands in the United States and Canada is not the happiest chapter in the history of either country. Both governments were frequently defrauded by speculators, and, more tragically, gullible citizens from eastern cities bought untold acres of land on the basis of fraudulent prospectuses. All too often towns with names like Happyvale and Pleasantville turned out to be completely unimproved swamps, though the advertising brochures showed charming engravings of full-skirted ladies promenading past opera houses along sycamore-lined boulevards. Even Charles Dickens was completely taken in and speculated heavily in worthless land in the area that eventually would develop around Cairo, Illinois. Dickens's measure of revenge, the description of New Eden in his novel *Martin Chuzzlewit*, is still the classic statement of American frontier fraud.

Sandusky itself started out more as bluff than as actual development. It was first carved out of the Firelands and platted in 1817, and the speculators who owned the townsite lost no time in convincing naive easterners to move there. As was usually the case in the Western Reserve, the speculators were from Connecticut, and Connecticut formed their market. In April, 1818, less than a year after the filing of the original plat, the following ditty appeared in the New Haven, Connecticut, *Journal*. It is meant to be sung to the tune of the folk song, "Henry Martin the Pirate."

The Fire-lands, embracing the present counties of Huron and Erie, was the next section carved off from her Western possessions by the State. During the Revolution, . . . nine towns were . . . plundered and laid waste, mostly by fire, and the inhabitants of one of them massacred. The sufferers, after the war appealed to the Legislature for relief, and, after several years discussion and delay, they were voted an appropriation of five hundred thousand acres, to be surveyed off from the western part of the Reserve, and distributed in proportion to their losses. The settlement of this district did not commence until about 1808, owing to Indian occupation and fear of hostilities.

*1812 History of
Sandusky County, Ohio*

Come on my good neighbors who live in the East,
　　Who wish for less winter and snow,
Come join with your friend, and we'll move to the West,
　　To *Sandusky New City* we'll go.

If commerce you choose, where it's not overdone,
　　(And many like trading, I know;)
Come join with your friend, and prepare to go on;
　　To *Sandusky New City* we'll go.

If fishing and fowling your fancy should take,
　　The half of each summer, or so,
To find rich employment on Erie's proud Lake;
　　To the *Bay of Sandusky* we'll go.

If farming should please us, and please us it must,
　　Where wealth, fame and luxury flow,
From tilling the soil as we find in the west,
　　To the *Land of Sandusky* we'll go.

Ye friends of good dairy, with your dairy wives,
　　Who like some fine cheeses and so,
To make up your fortune, and lead easy lives,
　　To *Sandusky Prairies* must go.

You who have no land, but have many fine boys,
  Tom, Andrew, John, Dick, Bob and Joe,
To get them good farms and increase your own joys,
  To the *Land of Sandusky* should go.

To charming Ohio, by thousands are gone,
  The best of our young men you know,
Who spurned dependence, by prospect led on,
  To the new world had spirit to go.

Then we who have daughters, young, blooming and fair,
  As roses and lilies can grow,
To marry them well and relieve tender care,
  To the *Land of Sandusky* will go.

Now Mary, dear Mary, what think you of this?
  Shall we move to the Westward or no?
I'll take a sweet kiss, while your lips answer yes,
  To *Sandusky New City* we'll go.

And to Sandusky they went, looking for "less winter and snow," "wealth, fame and luxury," and "easy lives." The first pioneers could not have been more disappointed in each of these particulars, but Sandusky ultimately did survive and prosper. Though initially the breaking up of the hard prairie sod did not result in the flow of wealth, fame, and luxury, once plowed, the soils of the Firelands proved rich and productive. And Sandusky itself was situated near the mouth of Sandusky Bay, a fine natural harbor that contributed to the development of commerce.

By 1849 the city boasted five thousand residents. In that year it was hit by the great cholera epidemic, the spread of the dreaded disease that wiped out major portions of the frontier in the 1830s through the 1850s. In the summer of 1849 cholera took the lives of over four hundred Sanduskians, and at the height of the epidemic more than half of the surviving residents of the city took to the woods in an effort to escape the disease. The local newspaper counseled optimism and cheerfulness and instructed its readership on how to avoid "unnecessary panic." It added, "We expect the report of interments will be pretty large today; but we hope it will be smaller tomorrow, if we live to make one."

As with Cleveland and other cities in the Western Reserve, most of Sandusky's early settlers were Connecticut Yankees, but as the town's industries developed in the 1830s and 1840s the population become more diversified, developing strong Irish and German bases. The opening of the Erie Canal in 1825 had a profound effect on the growth and diversification of the populations of Sandusky and other Great Lakes cities. For the first time, a relatively inexpensive all-water route from New York City was available, and as each wave of immigrants hit that city's waterfront, the groups quickly dispersed to the west. Ships from Buffalo provided the transport, and Scandinavians, Germans, Irish, and other ethnic groups distributed themselves to the many new population centers around the Lakes. Today the Great Lakes cities bear some evidence of the original influx by East Coast Yankees, but the succeeding overlay of immigrant populations proved more important in determining the cities' ultimate character.

One of the peculiar features of Sandusky's nineteenth-century history is the fact that the town was used as a base from which Americans could meddle in Canada's internal affairs; sometime later the Canadians used it to interfere with American concerns. A good deal of sympathy for the insurrectionists existed in the United States during the Canadian Rebellion of 1837. Although the American Revolution had been over for more than fifty years, the War of 1812 was still in mind, and many Americans both dreaded and held in contempt what they viewed as oppressive European despotism. During February, 1838, exiled rebel forces assembled in Sandusky to gather an invasion of Canada, and they were helped, concealed and provisioned by American sympathizers.

The rebel attack was two-pronged. One army of two hundred men proceeded across the ice and up the Detroit River to overwhelm Fort Malden at Amherstburg, while a force of a hundred and fifty rebels marched straight across the lake to occupy the area near Point Pelee. Both attacks were repelled short of their objectives. The first was easily turned back from the Detroit River. The second resulted in the Battle of the Ice. The invaders managed to capture the unfortified Pelee Island on February 26, but island residents fled and informed the British Army of what was up. The British counterattacked with a force of a thousand troops, and an engagement followed on the ice south of the island. The rebels managed to escape over ice too thin to support the British cavalry and artillery, but the Sandusky-based assault was over.

A more elaborate scheme involved Canadians in the American Civil War. During that conflict, Johnsons Island, which lies on the side of Sandusky Bay farthest from the city, was used as a prisoner-of-war camp, guarded by the heavily armed U.S.S. *Michigan*. Confederate agents operating out of Canada with the help of Canadian sympathizers brewed a bold plan for establishing a northern front to the Civil War. After seizing the *Michigan* and liberating the prisoners, they would exercise naval command of the Great Lakes, for the *Michigan* was the only vessel on the Lakes with significant armament. Relying on supplies clandestinely provided by Canadian supporters, they could then bombard and sack befuddled lake cities such as Cleveland and Lorain. The plotters almost pulled off their plan.

As a first step, a Captain Charles Cole arrived in Sandusky, posing as a bon vivant Philadelphia banker. To show his appreciation for the trials endured by the Union military, he frequently hosted parties attended by the officers of the *Michigan* and the Johnsons Island prison camp. He was

We left [central New York] by stage at an early hour in the morning and, after a long and tiresome day's ride, reached what was then called "Salt Point," afterwards Syracuse. We here embarked the next morning on the canal for Buffalo, a method of travel but recently introduced but exceedingly popular on account of its freedom from fatigue and because of the greater social advantages as well as being cheaper than by stage. . . .

After . . . three days and nights we reached Buffalo, then only a good-sized village, in time to take passage . . . on the good steamer *Niagara*, whereof Pease was master, bound for Detroit. We counted ourselves fortunate in having secured passage on this vessel, though the smallest on the line, yet first on account of her reliability as to time and ability to complete the round trip, Buffalo to Detroit and return, within a week.

H. Massey, 1828
(In a letter to the
Detroit Free Press)

permitted to ease the lives of the poor devils incarcerated on Johnsons Island by treating them to cigars. Inside each cigar wrapper was a piece of paper giving instructions as to what the prisoners should do when the uprising began.

On September 21, 1864, the body of the assault boarded the steamship *Philo Parsons* when it stopped at Amherstburg and Sandwich, Ontario, on its regular run from Detroit to Sandusky. Once out in Lake Erie, the Confederates captured the ship and dropped off the innocent passengers and most of the crew on Middle Bass Island. At its scheduled time, the *Parsons* arrived at Sandusky Bay but dallied off Cedar Point instead of continuing on to dock. That evening the good banker Cole was entertaining the crew of the *Michigan* at a shipboard champagne bash, the champagne having been previously drugged. Cole was to send off a rocket when the *Michigan*'s crew were all safely sleeping like kittens, and the pirates of the *Parsons* would then seize the *Michigan* and the prison camp.

The rocket was never fired. Half an hour before the party was to begin, the commander of the *Michigan* had learned the true identity of Cole and had had him arrested. After waiting in vain for the rocket signal, the crew of the *Parsons* reluctantly concluded that something had gone amiss. They took the ship across the lake to the sparsely populated Canadian shore, and the would-be leaders of the Great Lakes Fleet of the Confederate States of America escaped into the countryside.

For most of its history, Sandusky, along with most other Great Lakes small cities, has depended heavily on the Lakes. Its well-protected harbor in Sandusky Bay made it a major port in the nineteenth century. Commercial fishing has been a significant industry from the start: In fact, it has been claimed that in its heyday in the early 1880s Sandusky was the largest freshwater fishing center in the world. Fifteen hundred men were employed in the fishing business at that time. Also, the port's thriving caviar industry was unique on the Great Lakes. Sturgeon were caught and brought in, and the eggs were collected and processed. The caviar was then packed in 125-pound kegs and shipped to Europe, where it was repackaged into tiny jars and tins and sent back to the United States as fancy imported caviar with Russian names.

Today, Sandusky, which owes its existence to its harbor in the bay, is less oriented toward the Lakes than it was in days past. Other nearby cities—Cleveland, Lorain, Toledo—have outstripped it in terms of port facilities and water-related industry. The fishing has nearly disappeared, as it has most places on the Lakes, because of pollution, habitat loss, and other problems resulting in species depletion.

Sandusky is today a quiet town of square blocks and perpendicular streets, modest commercial and industrial attainments, and some 30,000 residents, few of whom carry on the town's Lake Erie tradition. But a good part of the Confederate Navy is still there in the tidy Civil War cemetery that overlooks the bay from Johnsons Island. And every once in a while one can find a car with a Connecticut license plate waiting to catch a ferry—a frail link with the town's seaboard origins, but a link nevertheless.

The Rise and Fall of the Copper Country

ONE hundred and forty years ago the tip of the Keweenaw Peninsula, the ragged spine of Michigan mainland that penetrates most deeply into Lake Superior, was an unexplored wilderness. Few people lived on the peninsula then, for the terrain was inhospitable to Indians and Europeans alike. But even at that time the land was not virgin. Pockmarking the entire peninsula were thousands of overgrown pits averaging twenty feet across and thirty feet deep—copper mines dug by an unknown people at an unknown time.

The Keweenaw Peninsula is still untamed and still resists transformation. The forests remain largely intact, though almost all the old-growth timber is gone. Except for the towns of Houghton and Hancock, the area is sparsely populated, and the wildlife dominates the land. But the evidence of past activity is richer now than it was in the 1830s, for in 1840 another round of copper-mining activity began to develop on the peninsula. It grew in fits and starts, but in 1910, at the height of the boom, nearly one hundred thousand people occupied the now largely vacant land.

The boom started when Douglass Houghton, a Detroit physician who was also Michigan's state geologist, explored the south shore of Lake Superior in 1840. He was deeply impressed with the copper resources there, and understandably so, since the Lake Superior copper deposits are a genuine freak of nature. The copper that Houghton discovered, and that had been mined by the earlier unknown culture millennia before, was pure copper that had formed in fissures in the ancient Precambrian rock. Houghton reported that a single blast could unearth boulders of the pure metal weighing up to forty pounds. The rumors arising from Houghton's reports had it that masses of pure copper were virtually lying around for the plucking, and they inspired the first of America's many prospecting frenzies, a precursor of the California Gold Rush of 1849. Hundreds of prospectors flocked to the Keweenaw wilderness to make their fortunes.

But copper is not like gold dust. It cannot be slung over the prospector's shoulder in a burlap bag, trotted down to a convenient agent, and sold for a tidy profit. Instead it must be mined in large quantities at minimal cost and then efficiently transported to a market. Almost everyone in the Copper Country went bust in the 1840s, individuals and corporations alike, for the veins of mass copper that had formed the basis of the aboriginal works simply could not provide the metal in sufficient quantities to make a nineteenth-century mining operation pay.

The few exceptions, the great bonanzas, kept interest alive in the early days. The first great

The attention of the earliest travelers was called to this mass of metallic copper by the natives of the country, and it has been repeatedly described by those who have visited it. The mass now lies in the bend of the westerly fork of the Ontonagon river. . . . The rugged character of the country is such, that it is but rarely visited, in proof of which I may state, that upon my visit to it, during the last year, I found broken chisels, where I had left them . . . nine years before, and even a mass of the copper, which . . . for the want of sufficient implements, I was compelled to abandon.

Douglas Houghton, 1840

Following our westerly direction to Point Keweenau, we find the dominion of Pluto established on a most magnificent scale. Not only is his energy displayed in the stern and rockbound coast, but in the lofty ranges of trap, which rise into rugged hills of from 400 to 900 feet above the lake. Within these are secreted, but scarcely concealed, those wonderful veins of native copper, here quarried rather than mined, in masses such as the world has nowhere else produced.

Bella Hubbard, 1887

strike was made at the Cliff Mine near the town of Eagle River. The mine hit a pure and profitable vein in the summer of 1846, and within two months the company had pulled out over four hundred tons of pure copper. Chunks of copper, chipped from the lode eight hundred feet underground, were piled along the dock at Eagle Harbor. Where it was necessary to separate metal from rock, the Indian technique was used: The ore was heated on a fire, and, when cold water was poured over it, the rock cracked away from the metal. From Eagle Harbor the copper was carried by ship to Sault Ste. Marie, portaged around the falls, and then loaded onto other ships for transport to Detroit and elsewhere.

By 1850 most of the early prospectors had gone home in disappointment, and the Keweenaw population was reduced to 750. By then it was clear that the Cliff Mine experience was exceptional and that profits in the Keweenaw mines would depend on new techniques. Starting in the early 1850s the companies went after a different kind of deposit, the amygdaloid ore. In these deposits the copper was also pure, but it was an igneous formation resulting in small nuggets imbedded in the surrounding bedrock. The amygdaloid ore had been largely ignored by the early miners, since extraction of the copper, usually 2 to 5 percent of the whole, was accomplished by crushing and then grinding the rock. But the amygdaloid deposits were extensive and relatively easy to detect, while mass copper finds, such as the one the Cliff Mine worked, were unreliable flukes, difficult to discover and almost always too small to yield a profit.

The amygdaloid miners were far more successful than the first wave of hopeful prospectors. Some of the mines reaped profits for decades. With this more modest boom in activity the population of the Keweenaw rose again. By 1860, it had reached 9,000. Another factor contributing to the population rise, as well as to the success of the mining activity generally, was the opening of the first set of locks at Sault Ste. Marie in 1855.

The following decade saw the development of the third generation of copper mining, the new wave that led to the true Keweenaw boom. In 1864 a Michigan miner named Edwin J. Hulbert sent a barrel of ore to his backers in Boston, hoping to convince them that it could be mined profitably. The material he sent them was Calumet conglomerate, a hard ore in which the copper and rock were thoroughly intermixed. In spite of the problem of separation, the conglomerate would prove to be by far the most common and profitable of the Keweenaw ores.

Hulbert's principal backer was a Boston Brahmin by the name of Quincy Adams Shaw, the cousin, close friend, and traveling companion of historian Francis Parkman, who dedicated *The Oregon Trail* to him. Shaw encouraged Hulbert to proceed but shortly afterwards became convinced that the miner was mismanaging the operation. He bought out Hulbert's interest and sent a partner out to Michigan to correct matters.

This partner, who became the dominant force on the peninsula, was Alexander Agassiz, the son of the naturalist Louis Agassiz. Agassiz was in his early thirties when he went west in 1867. He had inherited his father's scientific bent but had not yet managed to find a situation as a naturalist. He hoped to earn enough money in the mining operation to sustain himself in his chosen field. As things worked out, he remained president of the Calumet and Hecla Mining Company for thirty-nine years. During that time he established himself as a scientist and a philanthropic supporter of scientific endeavors. Agassiz managed to have a very full life by combining his interests in this way. In addition to mastering such specialized subjects as the flora and fauna of Lake Titicaca and the corals of the Maldive Islands, he found time to run the company with autocratic zest from Boston and to pay visits to his mine twice annually almost every year of his presidency.

In the year and a half that he lived in Michigan, Agassiz spent a great deal of Mr. Shaw's money. He had new shafts drilled and established stamp mills—for crushing ore—and refining plants a few miles away at Torch Lake. He planned corporate communities with the verve of Peter the Great filling the Baltic marshes. As a result his company began to emerge as the giant of the industry. By 1872, only eight years after Hulbert had sent his sample of ore to Boston, the Calumet and Hecla Mines were producing 65 percent of the copper in Michigan.

The census figures for Calumet Township show the Keweenaw boom in cold terms. The population in 1870 was 3,200; it rose to 8,300 in 1880, to 12,500 in 1890, to 26,000 in 1900, and peaked at 32,500 in 1910. Other townships on the peninsula also grew, under the stimulus of other profitable operations mining amygdaloid and conglomerate deposits, and in 1910 the Keweenaw population had reached almost 100,000.

But the census statistics do not show the frenzied pace of life that the mining industry spawned or the extraordinarily diverse population it attracted. Wherever a shaft went down, a corporate town grew. For decades the immigrants and the East Coast unemployed boarded ships in Buffalo and sailed up the waters of the Great Lakes to the Keweenaw. They worked in the mines and felled the timbers for the tunnels; they tended the stores and kept the bars; they attempted to farm in order to feed the towns they were building. Most of them started poor and stayed poor, and all too many perished in grisly mining accidents. They brought their languages, entertainments, food specialties, and customs. They built company houses on company land or rented houses from the company; they read books from its libraries, used its hospitals, and sent their children to its schools. But, at least in the townships under Agassiz's authority, they built their own shops, theaters, saloons, and whorehouses.

The Keweenaw population during this period was among the most ethnically diverse in the world. In 1870, two-thirds of Calumet Township's population was foreign born. The 1900 census showed that 28,000 of Houghton County's 66,000 residents had been born outside the United States, and, of those, over 1,000 people were counted in each of ten different ethnic groupings.

In 1872 the Northwestern extended its road from Green Bay to Menominee and Escanaba. This made a through line from Marquette and Ishpeming to Chicago. Also in 1872 the Marquette, Houghton & Ontonagon Railway had been completed to L'Anse, at the head of Keweenaw Bay, a distance of sixty-two miles. There was also a narrow-gauge road, twelve miles in length, running from Hancock northeasterly to the Calumet & Hecla copper mine. These, I believe, were the only railroads in operation at that time.

John Longyear, 1873

51

The Finns headed the list with over 7,000 people, followed in order by the English (mainly Cornish), French Canadians, English-speaking Canadians, "Austrians" (actually Slovenians and Croatians), Italians, Germans, Swedes, Irish, and Norwegians. Also counted were a lesser number of Poles, Scots, Hungarians, French, Swiss, Russians, Chinese, Danes, various Asians, Australians, Belgians, Bohemians, Greeks, Dutch, and West Indians.

Each major group tended to keep its own language and customs, and different stores and commercial establishments catered to specialized ethnic requirements. Generally each group had its own church, which held services in its native language. And benevolent associations were established to promote the interests of their own minorities. In the larger towns, such as Red Jacket, home-country national and religious holidays were constantly being celebrated.

But even considering the sometimes frenzied rate of growth and the population diversity, a mining community is a ghost town in embryo. Sooner or later the deposits will give out or become inaccessible, and the dregs will no longer compete with supplies elsewhere. The Keweenaw suffered a lingering death. Although the area continued to expand until 1910, and although the two world wars somewhat revived the slumping economy after that, the mining industry steadily declined after the turn of the century. Towns such as Calumet have shown a drop in population in every census since 1910.

The Depression had a savage effect on the region. One New Deal official declared the Copper Country the hardest hit area of its size in the country in 1934. During that period the Calumet and Hecla Company started selling off its houses for five dollars apiece, and even at that price many people could not afford to buy. Finally, in 1968, the few remaining mines were closed permanently by a strike. In that same year the Calumet and Hecla Mining Company became a division of a corporate conglomerate, the Universal Oil Products Company. So ended the peninsula's second surge of copper-mining activity. Every so often nowadays rumors circulate on Keweenaw that "they" may open the mines again. Maybe they will someday; plenty of copper still remains in the ground. But copper is plentiful elsewhere, too, and it is more easily obtainable by the less-expensive pit-mining methods.

Today, the Keweenaw is little more tamed and transformed by the nineteenth-century copper industry than it had been earlier by the aboriginal mining that had taken place millennia before. Nowadays people assume they can gain control over any piece of land and at least temporarily force it to respond to their schemes. But perhaps the stubborn intransigence of the Keweenaw to yield itself to short-range human interests offers a lesson: In this case, the land is best met on its own terms.

The Monarchy on Beaver Island

BEAVER ISLAND can be one of the quietest places in the world. Few tourists visit during the true tourist season, though some visitors do come to the island to see the fall colors and, later, to stalk the island's deer. Yet at one time, when it hosted a bizarre conflict of clashing cultures and ambitions, this peaceful island was the scene of the most concentrated turmoil on the Great Lakes.

Beaver Island lies in the middle of the northernmost part of Lake Michigan where the long lake bends eastward toward the Straits of Mackinac. Settlement began in the same fashion as it did on dozens of other islands on the Lakes. Fishermen started to use the nearly perfect harbor at the north end of the island as a base for their operations. By the 1840s two commercial establishments were in operation at the harbor. One of these was a dock at which cordwood was sold to steamers; the location was ideal for commerce with ships coming from or bound for the Straits. At the south end of the island was a second small community, which had its own general store and a cooper who made the barrels that fishermen used to pack their salted-down catches. In the mid-1840s Beaver Island showed every sign of drifting through the decades without ever making a ripple in United States' history.

But in August, 1846, in Wisconsin, James J. Strang had a vision. The Lord appeared to him and instructed him to move his people to the uninhabited islands of Lake Michigan. Strang's people were an offshoot colony of Mormons who had left the main body of the Saints when Strang, in a power struggle with Brigham Young, failed to gain control of the population. Strang had moved his people up to Voree, Wisconsin, from Nauvoo, Illinois, but now the Lord was telling him to move again.

Strang's vision had a practical basis. Throughout their brief history, the Mormons had been persecuted and terrorized, and Mormon leaders realized that putting geographical distance between themselves and those they called the gentiles was the only course that could lead to the peaceful development of the Mormon community. For Young and the main Mormon settlement, that decision meant undertaking the almost unimaginable hardships of the trek to the Great American Desert, which they began in the same year that Strang had his vision. For Strang, isolation would be accomplished by following the Lord's injunction and moving his people to the uninhabited islands of Lake Michigan.

After looking at the possibilities, Strang decided on Beaver Island, and the next summer he started to move his people from Voree. During the winter of 1847–48, eighteen Mormons lived on the island; the following winter, they numbered sixty-two. After that year, the colony experienced more rapid growth.

Strang would have saved everybody a great deal of trouble if he had followed the Lord's instructions more literally and chosen an island that was indeed uninhabited. But Beaver Island was the largest island in the lake, one of the few large enough to support a community on the scale envisioned by Strang, and in any event the pattern of settlement there would have been duplicated on virtually any large island he might have chosen.

Trouble erupted right from the start. The gentile inhabitants of Beaver Island—who probably numbered little more than a hundred when the Mormon immigration started—found the Mormons to be self-righteous and arrogant. They disliked the new settlers' religious doctrines, and they loathed such cultural practices as polygamy. The Mormons were experiencing the same hatred they had known in Nauvoo, from which they had been driven, but with one difference: Within a few years the Mormons far outnumbered the gentiles on Beaver Island.

By 1850 the gentiles decided to take the offensive and to celebrate the nation's seventy-fourth birthday by roughing up the Mormons on the Fourth of July. The gentile men met at Peter McKinley's general store on Whiskey Point, across the bay from the main Mormon settlement, to plan the assault. They did not know that the Mormons had brought a small artillery piece to the island for their defense. The Mormons heard about the meeting at McKinley's store and lobbed a cannonball across the waters of the bay to Whiskey Point. That shot was the end of the battle.

The incident put an end to any pretense of equality between the two populations. Four days later, on July 8, 1850, James J. Strang had himself crowned king and in his coronation address proclaimed his intention to rule the island and its inhabitants in a spirit of "meekness and truth and righteousness." Later the same day, he revealed another of his directives from God: The Lord had designated "the Islands of the Great Lakes as an inheritance for the Saints, delegating to the King the power of apportioning the land among His people."

First Beaver Island and the islands of Lake Michigan and now the islands of the Great Lakes—Strang was clearly displaying an imperial itch, recognized as such by civil officials, up to and including President Millard Fillmore. The president, having heard complaints about Strang during a visit to Detroit, ordered an investigation. In the spring of 1851, the U.S.S. *Michigan*—the same ship that later figured in the Confederate plan to gain control of the Great Lakes—arrived at St. James, the newly named principal village of the island. Strang and his most important courtiers were arrested and sent to Detroit.

They were charged with treason, counterfeiting, mail robbery, and trespassing upon public lands. The last charge was certainly valid—Strang, having received his mandate from God, saw no reason to comply with federal land-disposal laws and simply presented newly arrived settlers with tracts of land as "inheritances." Nevertheless, Strang personally conducted the defense, and all the defendants were acquitted.

Although the Mormon leadership suffered no consequences from its encounters with federal law, 1851 was a year of constant tension and disorder on the island. The tone was set in February, when King Strang revealed yet another divine pronouncement. God told Strang:

Let your fear be upon all men; and the terror of you upon your enemies; for this is the day of the vengeance of the Lord, and of your recompence upon your enemies. Arise and thrash, for I will make thy power iron; the tread of thy foot shall crush: thou shalt break in pieces many people, and shall consecrate their spoil unto God, and their dominion to the Lord of the whole earth.

The King had changed his tune considerably in the seven months since he had pledged to rule in a spirit of meekness.

The Beaver Island gentiles had no doubt about whose spoil would be consecrated unto God, or into whose hands God would ultimately direct the spoil. Nor did any question remain in their minds about the identity of those to be thrashed.

In the following months a number of turbulent encounters between the two populations did take place. Some involved gunfire, and at least one person, a gentile, was slain during the period of open conflict. The gentiles had been hopeful when Strang was arraigned, but, following the acquittal, new Mormons continued to arrive on the island, making the population imbalance ever more extreme, and the gentiles beat a retreat. By the winter of 1851–52, most of the gentile population had moved to the southern end of the island, putting as much distance as they could between themselves and the Mormons in St. James.

But this self-imposed segregation was not good enough. In the middle of 1852 the king issued an edict addressed directly to the gentiles: "Leave by November 10." As by sheer dint of numbers the gentiles had no practical choice, they complied, and the Mormons had the island entirely to themselves.

For the next three and a half years, King James Strang ruled Beaver Island without hindrance. Each new Mormon family arriving on the island was assigned by the king a tract of land to clear and till. An 1852 map shows the island neatly parceled off and overlaid by a grid of straight roads; over the years, the names of families were carefully penned in to show the assignments of land. No disinterested census exists which might indicate how large the population became. In 1854 the Mormons claimed that over twenty-six hundred residents lived on the island, but this figure may have been inflated to impress outsiders with the degree to which they had taken hold.

The settlement's economy was based largely on agriculture. Gradually the trees came down, and much of the island was covered with neatly fenced rectangular fields surrounding tidy farmsteads and orchards. King Strang not only directed the clearing and settling of the countryside, but he and his principal aides ran every aspect of life in St. James with strict discipline. All the details of social intercourse, from the rituals at the tabernacle to permissible forms of dress, were strictly regulated. Perhaps the king's greatest interest was in the printing shop he established early in his reign; from there he published a newspaper and innumerable propaganda tracts, thereby maintaining control, to a great degree, over what was thought about and discussed on the island.

When [the Mormons] failed [to convert those on the island not of the faith] they became angry and the Mormon elders said that they would see that "every dog of a gentile left the island." Mr. Geer, my grandfather, . . . put his family and what supplies he was allowed to take into a small boat and sailed away . . . And the wind, as Master Mariner, took him to the shores of Pine River . . . Mr. Geer made a clearing and built a small log cabin . . . As spring came he made a garden, planting some vegetable seeds he had brought with him. He also tapped trees for sap and made a quantity of maple syrup. But just when he was beginning to see some results from his labors the Mormons came to the mainland and drove him away again, not allowing him to take his maple syrup nor any of his garden produce with him.

Mrs. Harrison Bedford,
Charlevoix, Michigan

Still, King James Strang was not content with his realm. In 1852 he pulled off a rather un-monarchical master stroke. On election day in November he announced his candidacy for the Michigan state legislature; by the end of the day, he had received all of the island's 165 votes. The district was huge geographically but had very few people in it, and Strang's constituency was sufficient to elect him. The king remained a state legislator until his death.

He also began to carry out the broad mandate of his revelations. He sent out colonists to the neighboring Fox Islands, to nearby areas of the mainland, and even to Drummond Island in Lake Huron at the mouth of the St. Mary's River.

But while the king and his colony were prospering, his enemies were biding their time, waiting for the opportunity to strike. The gentiles' bitterness with respect to the dislocations they suffered is easy to understand. Some families were first forced out of St. James and resettled on the south end of the island only to be ordered to leave the island altogether. Those who had settled on the mainland near the site of Charlevoix were forced to move yet a third time when the Saints established a colony there.

The gentiles got their chance for revenge in the summer of 1856. On June 16, Strang was shot and wounded by two of his own subjects. He was immediately removed from the island and taken back to Voree, his settlement in Wisconsin. About the first of July, the sheriff of Mackinac County informed the now leaderless Mormons that they had settled illegally on public land, in some cases usurping the private land of others, and that they would have to leave the island immediately. Before they could react, armed vigilante parties arrived from the mainland on several chartered ships. They herded the Saints aboard and took them off to Chicago. On July 9, the United States's only king died in Voree, Wisconsin. He died without a kingdom, and his subjects once again found themselves homeless and dispersed in an inhospitable land.

Queens of the Waters

FUR TRADERS, navies, industrialists, pleasure-seekers, and international merchants have set their boats and ships upon the waters of the Great Lakes, each in their own time, each for their own interests. In every era, a few ships have won the nod of history.

The first queen of the Great Lakes, and grandmother of all the rest, was the *Griffin*. She was built in 1679 by French explorer Robert Cavelier, Sieur de La Salle, and was the first sailing vessel on the Great Lakes.

Every modern depiction of the *Griffin* is different. She is shown variously with two or three masts, flying anywhere from three to six sails. One sketch shows a great prancing griffin at the bow, balanced at the stern by an equally great eagle with wings flung out wide.

Whatever she looked like, we know something about the ship's brief history. She was built at the eastern end of Lake Erie, at that time the closest possible site to the French settlements on the St. Lawrence. Not for 150 years would Niagara Falls cease to be an impassable barrier to navigation between Lake Erie and Lake Ontario. On August 7, 1679, the *Griffin* set sail for the west end of Lake Erie, and eventually La Salle and his crew sailed her to Washington Island, off the Door Peninsula, where she was filled with a load of furs.

On September 18, forty-two days after she departed from the head of the Niagara River, La Salle watched the *Griffin* sail away from Washington Island on her return trip; he himself stayed on to explore the Green Bay area. The *Griffin* was never heard from again.

Her career was an inauspicious beginning for Great Lakes waterborne commerce—total productive life span: forty-two days; total payload delivered: zero.

Nobody knows what happened to the *Griffin*. Her crew may have scuttled her to stay in the northwest and seek their fortunes in the fur trade, or she may have broken up in a storm. No one has made a definitive list of "authenticated" sites of the wreck of the *Griffin*, but they range all the way from Washington Island to Buffalo.

Shortly after stumbling into war with Great Britain in 1812, the United States became aware of a particular vulnerability along her northern Great Lakes frontier. The government therefore decided to build a navy. Late in the first year of the war, a makeshift shipyard was established at Misery Bay, on the Presque Isle Peninsula across from the site of today's city of Erie. The conditions there were wild and formidable, but, by midsummer of 1813, six small ships had been completed and launched. The two largest, the *Lawrence* and the *Niagara*, were too heavy to pass over the bar at the mouth of the bay. They had to be lightened, secured to empty tanks called camels, and hauled out onto the open lake.

These six ships, along with three very small preexisting vessels, constituted America's Great Lakes fleet. It was entrusted to a 28-year-old officer from Rhode Island named Oliver Hazard Perry.

Perry's flagship was the *Lawrence,* named after an American naval captain, James Lawrence, who had been killed in action earlier that year attempting to lift the British blockade of Boston. Lawrence gained instant immortality with his last words, which he uttered as he was being carried, dying, from his quarterdeck: "Don't give up the ship." Perry had a large flag made, bearing this motto, which he hung from the mast of his flagship.

The British meanwhile had built up their own fleet at similarly improvised shipyards along the Detroit River. The British Great Lakes Navy, under the command of Captain Robert Barclay, had only six ships, but, in terms of firepower, it was slightly superior to the American fleet.

The battle of Lake Erie, the only significant naval engagement in the history of the Great

*Lake Huron rolls, Superior sings
in the rooms of her ice water mansion.
Old Michigan steams like a young man's
    dreams;
the islands and bays are for sportsmen.
And farther below Lake Ontario
takes in what Lake Erie can send her,
and the iron boats go as the mariners all know
with the Gales of November remembered.*

*The legend lives on from the Chippewa on down
of the big lake they called "Gitche Gumee."
"Superior," they said, "never gives up her dead
when the Gales of November come early!"*

Gordon Lightfoot
*"The Wreck of the
Edmund Fitzgerald"*

Lakes, occurred on September 10, in the waters off the Bass Islands in the western end of the lake. The *Lawrence* was quickly crippled, and Perry did in fact give up the ship. Striking his colors, he escaped to the *Niagara* in a rowboat with four sailors and his 13-year-old brother. He rejoined the battle in his new flagship and within a few hours vanquished Barclay and the British. Thus the *Niagara* became the undisputed queen of the Great Lakes.

Perry's niche in the pages of Bartlett's *Familiar Quotations* was earned by the report to his superior he wrote shortly after the battle: "We have met the enemy and they are ours: two ships, two brigs, one schooner and one sloop." The British had casualties of forty dead and one hundred wounded; the Americans had thirty dead, and also one hundred wounded.

In 1913, on the centennial of the battle, the remains of the *Niagara* were rescued from an underwater grave at Misery Bay. From the intact keel timbers and other portions of the hull that were reasonably well preserved, a complete reconstruction of the brig was made. Today the reconstructed *Niagara* rests on sixteen concrete props on Erie's main street not far from the waterfront, looking as uncomfortable as a fish out of water.

Throughout the nineteenth century, shipping on the Lakes developed and changed; steel hulls replaced wood, steamships edged out sailing vessels, and propellers took over from side paddles. At the very end of the century, starting in 1888, a distinctive new kind of ship appeared on the Lakes —the whalebacks, the brainchild of a Scots-Canadian named Alexander McDougall. For the time, the whalebacks were probably the most advanced ships anywhere in the world.

The last of the whalebacks, the *Meteor*, is today permanently moored as a floating museum at Superior, Wisconsin. At first glance she looks like the world's largest cigar—a 366-foot-long cigar, to be precise. McDougall's insight was that a rounded hull lying low in the water would be more seaworthy and have for its size a greater cargo capacity than the conventional high-sided steamships of the day. He therefore designed the whaleback to have a flat bottom and rounded, bulging sides that curved in above the waterline, leaving space for only a narrow, flattened deck running the length of the ship. The hull ended in a snoutlike point at both bow and stern, which earned the whalebacks the nickname "pigboats." Fully laden, the ships came closer to plowing through the water than riding above it. Since waves broke across the decks, the superstructure containing the pilothouse and accommodations was usually elevated on turrets at the stern.

Forty-three of these hulls were launched in various forms between 1888 and 1898, most of them from McDougall's yard in Superior. About half were unpowered barges, designed to be towed behind other ships. One, the *Christopher Columbus*, was a passenger ship, built as an excursion vessel for Chicago's Columbian Exposition of 1893. The remainder were bulk cargo carriers, each with a capacity for some five thousand tons of iron ore, grain, or stone.

The *Meteor* was launched on April 25, 1896, as the *Frank Rockefeller*, and for the next seventy-four years, assuming a variety of names and carrying a variety of cargoes, she traveled up and down the Lakes. She survived much in the course of her service, including the terrible Great Lakes November storms. Weather conditions around the Great Lakes are very unstable in the fall; large low-pressure systems develop quickly and move in fast to produce the powerful storms.

As the twentieth century progressed, the *Meteor* grew smaller and smaller in relation to her sisters on the Lakes, but she survived her increasingly apparent obsolescence to an amazing degree. Still, the modernity of the space age finally caught up with her. The largest of today's behemoths have a carrying capacity of ten times that of the *Meteor*. In 1970 the *Meteor*'s operators, Cleveland Tankers, announced that she would be taken out of service and scrapped, since they assumed that she could not be sold. But the people of Superior, the *Meteor*'s original home town, expressed so much interest in the old vessel that the company donated her to the city, and on September 11, 1972, she arrived—under tow—to start her new career as a museum.

For every sailor who has earned a living on the ships of the Great Lakes, hundreds have sailed upon the waters for pleasure alone. Every conceivable craft has made every conceivable kind of journey on the river of lakes. Sailboat racing—compared by one observer to the thrill of standing in a cold shower tearing up twenty-dollar bills—has long been popular on the Great Lakes, and its most prestigious event, the race that determines the queen of the Great Lakes sailing fleet, is the Canada's Cup series. This race, which has been held twelve times since its establishment in 1896, involves both the United States and Canada. A number of elimination races are held in each country, and the two winning boats then represent their respective nations in a series of match races.

In 1972 the American yacht *Dynamite* dislodged the cup from the elegant halls of the Royal Canadian Yacht Club in Toronto, where it had rested comfortably for eighteen years. In 1975 the Canadians mounted a challenge to bring it back.

The elimination action took place during the summer of that year. After forty races the American judging committee selected *Golden Dazy* to be the defender against the Canadian challenger, *Marauder*. The boats were well matched, especially since one rule of the race restricts the size, and implicitly the speed, of the contending yachts.

Dazy won the first three races and *Marauder* won the fourth, a two-hundred-mile workout on Lake Huron in fifty-mile-an-hour winds. After four races the point score was *Dazy* 3, *Marauder* 2, the long race having counted twice as much as the short ones. Four points were needed to win the series; *Marauder* had to win the fifth race to stay in contention.

The race started badly for *Marauder,* as *Dazy* crossed the line in front by over thirty seconds, an enormous advantage that is difficult to overcome. But the Canadians patiently took advantage

A strong nor'wester's blowin', Bill!
Hark! don't ye hear it roar now?
Lord help 'em, how I pities them
Unhappy folks on shore now!

The wind's nortwest and a-blowing all night,
See them big seas roll with their bonnets all
*   white!*
And far o'er our starb'rd rail
Is half a hundred sail.
Hooray! For a sail down the lakes.

of every puff and shift in the light, fluky wind, and *Marauder* rounded the first turning buoy three minutes ahead. Now it was *Dazy*'s turn to gradually close the distance; at the last turning mark, she was only a minute behind. Both boats flew every square inch of colorful nylon sail they could for the last downwind leg to the finish line. Almost imperceptibly *Dazy* drew closer, finally passing the Canadian boat, and, after twenty miles of racing, crossed the finish line sixteen seconds ahead.

The *Golden Dazy* was built by Gougeon Brothers boatyard of Bay City, Michigan, using a process of wood lamination developed there. She was a fine-looking craft, but her beauty was entirely fortuitous. The wooden construction technique was chosen not on an esthetic basis but because it yields a strong yet extraordinarily light hull, a feature that translates into speed. Clearly, *Dazy* was a pure racing machine.

Golden Dazy was by no means the largest, most expensive, or even the fastest sailboat on the Great Lakes in the year of her triumph, and she was certainly not the most versatile. She was designed and created for the single purpose of defending the Canada's Cup. Having done so successfully, she indisputably proved herself a queen.

The *Stewart J. Cort* was the first of the thousand-foot-long lake carriers made possible by the opening of the rebuilt and lengthened Poe Lock at the Soo in 1970. Prior to the opening of this lock and the arrival of the supercarriers, modern Great Lakes ships ran about 750 feet in length and could carry about thirty thousand tons of cargo. Ships of the *Cort*'s generation can haul about fifty thousand tons.

The lake freighter is a specialized ship developed to meet conditions found on these waters. It is quite different from the usual ocean-going cargo ship; when one occasionally sees in a distant salt-water port a lake freighter that somehow has strayed into ocean trade, there still is no question as to where and how she began her career. The flat sides; wheelhouse in the bows; long, open deck; engine room in the stern—all these are the marks recognized the world over, of the Great Lakes freighter.

James P. Barry
The Fate of the Lakes

In her general appearance, the *Cort* bears the traditional laker look that evolved with the decline of the whalebacks around the turn of the century. Ships designed for operation on the Lakes do not have to contend with the stronger forces of the oceans, so seahandling characteristics can be downplayed in order to accommodate larger payloads. Great Lakes ships have vertical sides that are carried well forward into the bow, and the bow itself is a blunt, vertical leading edge. These boxy vessels have none of the graceful flare in the bow that characterizes ocean-going ships, or "salties," as they are called on the Lakes. Another characteristic of the laker is the pilothouse on a superstructure right at the bow which allows the captain a close view for maneuvering through tight locks and crowded ports.

The *Cort* is well adapted to moving iron ore from Lake Superior to the steel mills on the Lower Lakes, the activity which lies at the heart of the Great Lakes shipping industry. Between the superstructures at her bow and the stern stretch hundreds of feet of cargo deck. Spaced evenly along the centerline are more than a dozen hatches through which the ore is poured into the enormous cavity below. Like most modern Great Lakes ships, the *Cort* is a self-unloader. A system of conveyor belts makes it possible for her to unload her cargo in a matter of hours.

The *Cort*'s reign as queen of the carriers was destined to be brief. Other supercarriers have joined her, and more are on the way. But she unquestionably earned her place in history as the first of the thousand-footers, introducing new life into the Great Lakes shipping industry.

THE LEGACY

Protecting the Rural Shorelines

THE SHORELINES that border the Great Lakes and their islands total over eleven thousand miles. A very small proportion of the total lies within cities and towns. Most of the shoreline areas are in the countryside. But with respect to the Great Lakes, "countryside" is too broad a term to be descriptive. Countryside shorelines along the Lakes range from the drabbest of embankments adjoining railroad tracks to some of the most rugged wilderness on the North American continent.

No one person could inspect all eleven thousand miles in a lifetime, but lovers of the Great Lakes make a valiant effort. Perhaps the fact that a shoreline is so distinct and easily definable inspires in modern explorers the urge to see every foot of it, to tramp every beach, to land on every island. Shoreline buffs log hundreds of hours in what might seem to be aimless wanderings to those who do not share the compulsion to explore. But Great Lakes wanderers are easily rewarded and rarely disappointed, for these diverse shores always present something interesting to see. Perhaps the joys of discovery seem a little strained to the uninitiated, and the entertainment somewhat simpleminded, but the impulse to do or see "because it is there" has never been rational. You either have it or you don't.

Traditionally the term "wilderness" has inspired fear and visions of ferocious beasts, oppressive and impenetrable forests, and dangers of all kinds surrounding the unwary traveler as closely as the shell encases the turtle. But, increasingly, we find that we need wilderness: We need to visit it if we can and to let our imaginations dwell on it if our bodies are detained elsewhere.

Among the most eloquent definitions of the rather vague term "wilderness" are, oddly enough, those found in the United States Code of federal statutes. The Wilderness Act of 1964 refers to a wilderness as "an area where the earth and its community of life are untrammeled by man, where man himself is a visitor who does not remain," and as a region that "generally appears to have been affected primarily by the forces of nature, with the imprint of man's works substantially unnoticeable."

Yet any definition of a specific wilderness area must be interpreted within the context of the local geography. Very few lands around the Great Lakes, for instance, are completely free of signs of human activity. During the nineteenth and early twentieth centuries, the whole region was thoroughly logged over, and very little virgin timber is left. Still in many areas the feeling of wildness remains or has been regained. Ultimately, perhaps, a definition of wilderness must rest on the frame of mind that the land induces. Under that stipulation, even a rock can be a wilderness. For a decade the only lands in the state of Wisconsin that were protected under the federal Wilderness Act of 1964 were three barren islands, with a total area of less than twenty acres, in Lake Michigan. Thousands of these rocks are scattered throughout the Great Lakes, and each is a bit of wilderness in spirit if not in name, since each can provide the rare visitor with a moment of solitude.

But the large Great Lakes wilderness areas are concentrated around Lake Superior and the northeastern shores of Lake Huron. By far the largest single wild area is Canada's Pukaskwa National Park, which occupies the hump of land that bulges out from the northeast shore of Lake Superior between Marathon and Michipicoten. This tract, totaling hundreds of square miles, is so wild and impenetrable that it is seldom visited. Earnest backpackers or canoeists attempting to find maps of the park discover that detailed maps do not exist; they are advised against venturing into the area without an Ojibway guide.

A more accessible but still remote wilderness region is Isle Royale National Park, also on Lake Superior. Although it lies off the Canadian shore, Isle Royale is part of the state of Michigan; legend has it that Benjamin Franklin negotiated for its inclusion within the United States as part of the Paris Treaty of 1783, because he had heard that the island was rich in copper. Whether or not the tale is true, its substance is correct; evidence of prehistoric copper mining similar to that on the Keweenaw Peninsula exists on the island.

In the 1930s, Isle Royale was included within the National Park System; ever since, it has been managed with an eye toward keeping development to a minimum. Lodges have been built at both ends, but in the forty-mile area that separates the two facilities only a few small campgrounds and an occasional dock give evidence of human intervention.

Physically, Isle Royale has much in common with the Canadian north shore and the Keweenaw Peninsula. It is composed of the same hard Precambrian rock and clearly shows the effects of the glaciation process. The island lies in a northeast–southwest direction aligned with the mainland shore and consists of a series of parallel ridges that run along its length. These ridges were formed by the Pleistocene glaciers advancing to the southwest and then retreating to the northeast. Between these ridges are deep valleys filled with swamps, ponds, lakes, and bogs.

Isle Royale is divisible into two distinct portions. At the eastern end, the long ridges and valleys dip under the waters of Lake Superior and form a series of deep inlets along the shoreline— some several miles long and only a few hundred yards wide—separated by narrow steep-spined points. At this end of the island a visitor is seldom far from the lake, and the ambiance is distinctly aquatic. The trees are mainly conifers. At its western end the island bulges out, and the sequence of ridges and valleys is much less pronounced. The tree cover is principally maple, and the feeling conveyed is similar to that of the mainland rather than a northwoods island. A hike from one end of the island to the other leads a backpacker gently from one natural system to another, though many animals—from whiskeyjack to moose—inhabit both.

Until about 1949 the moose were the undisputed rulers of Isle Royale. In that year a pack of wolves crossed the winter ice from the Canadian north shore, and since then the two populations— approximately twenty-five wolves and several hundred moose—have established a natural equilibrium. The wolves trim the aged and weak animals out of the moose herds, thus keeping the

The bathing in the pure waters of the Strait at [Mackinac] is truly delightful, affording health and vigor to the human frame . . . Summer visitors annually flock to [Sault Sainte Marie] and the Lake Superior country for health and pleasure . . . On the North Shore [of Lake Superior], Canada side, are several fine trout fishing resorts, from fifteen to sixty miles from the Saut [sic], where Indians or half-breeds with their canoes have to be employed, often camping out for several days. . . .

John Disturnell, 1874

moose numbers from exceeding the island's carrying capacity. At the same time, the limited availability of prey—a full-grown, healthy moose is more than a match for a wolf—tends to keep the wolf population fairly constant.

The relationship between the moose and wolves on Isle Royale has provided an ideal natural laboratory for scientists interested in animal behavior. Because the species are contained on the island, their range is well defined and easily discernible. Few complicating variables need be taken into account. For example, no deer on the island compete with the moose for forage or provide alternative large prey for the wolves. And, since the regulations of the National Park Service strictly prohibit hunting, the effects of man are minimal.

The great wilderness parks such as Isle Royale or Pukaskwa are the exception along the Great Lakes shoreline. More common are smaller parks designed to serve as an introduction to the Great Lakes region. An almost limitless variety of parks exists around the Lakes, operated by every level of political jurisdiction. Some are magnificent creations carefully planned to highlight the natural landscape; others are nasty affairs that mutilate the landforms they were theoretically created to protect.

A visit to Canada's Point Pelee National Park is almost guaranteed to invigorate the spirit. Point Pelee is a sandbar that juts some ten miles down into the western end of Lake Erie. The western face of the bar is a beach, the top stabilized with vegetation, and the area behind the bar to the east is an extensive stretch of shallows that provide prime marsh habitat for waterfowl. The winds and currents of Lake Erie constantly work on the tip of this peninsula, and from the air Point Pelee looks like a finely sharpened dart cutting through the waters of the lake.

Point Pelee is the southernmost tip of the Canadian mainland. That fact, together with the moderating influence of the surrounding water of Lake Erie, accounts for the presence of vegetation and ecological communities not found elsewhere in Canada.

The national park has been developed with an eye toward serving various kinds of recreational demands without changing in any way the natural phenomena on the point. On the marshy side, for example, a boardwalk and tower have been built to enable visitors to look for waterfowl and aquatic life. Along the wooded spine of the peninsula are nature trails for those who prefer to scrutinize upland flora and fauna. Birdwatchers in particular favor these trails.

The miles-long beach on the west side of the point is popular with swimmers and sunbathers during the summer. Picnic tables, parking areas, and access points are discreetly located so as not to overwhelm the landscape. The determined beachcomber can wander out for several miles to the very tip of the peninsula to where the vegetation gives way and only the pioneer beach species punctuate the sand. Cars are forbidden on the sandy point, but a miniature train takes the less ambitious visitors out to the end.

The natural beauties and wildness of [Mackinac] island, its situation, enthroned at the apex of the peninsula of Michigan and embracing magnificent views of water and island, its lake breezes and pure cold air, and the excellence of its whitefish and trout, have long made it one of the most attractive of watering places. The proposal to conserve it as a national park is worthy of its character, and it is to be hoped that thus its natural beauties, and what remains of its woods, will be preserved forever to the nation.

Bella Hubbard, 1887

Point Pelee is a model of what a public park can be. Clearly a prime consideration in the design was the protection of land and wildlife resources; visitor use was patterned around that priority rather than vice versa. The government took great care to provide visitors with a wide variety of experiences, and planned space intelligently so as to make a visit pleasant and enjoyable.

Not all parks are laid out with these criteria in mind. If Point Pelee exemplifies successful park design, "Parking Lot Duneless State Park," more formally known as Indiana Dunes State Park, occupies the other end of the spectrum. This once-lovely land at the south end of Lake Michigan has been run as a park since the 1920s by the state of Indiana, which has lavished upon it the same degree of love that a mongoose gives to a cobra. The sand dunes after which the park was named have been replaced by a seemingly endless series of parking lots. So many campsites, roads, and facilities are squeezed into the nearby campground that it seems crowded even in the absence of visitors. And everywhere one looks are signs of the strong-arm variety: "No parking," "Do not walk on the grass," "Changing of clothing in the rest rooms is prohibited."

Indiana has fallen into the common trap of trying to accommodate too many people—or, to be precise, too many automobiles—in too small a space. The state has compounded the effects of this error by failing to spend the money, imagination, and effort needed to make a crowded park as pleasing as possible. The state justifies the result by citing as its sacred duty the opening up of the Lake Michigan shoreline to as many residents as possible, adding that performance of this duty inevitably results in a certain amount of deterioration and crowding. This argument is offered by the same state whose political leaders have for decades responded coolly—and often with downright hostility—to the proposal that a federal lakeshore area be established along stretches of the Indiana Dunes. Indiana's public officials quite apparently prefer to see Lake Michigan's shoreline dedicated exclusively to industrial use and port facilities.

Between the extremes of Point Pelee and "Parking Lot Duneless" are hundreds of developed parks on the lakes, managed under federal, state, provincial, and local auspices. Taken together they satisfy almost every recreational taste. Some conservationists, for example, have a special fondness for recycled buildings. They would be interested to know that when the United States Coast Guard abandoned Split Rock Lighthouse on the Minnesota north shore of Lake Superior, it turned the buildings over to the state for use as a park. Standing on a cliff nearly two hundred feet above the lake, the lighthouse has the distinction of being at the highest elevation above sea level of any building in the United States: Before it was retired the million-candlepower lamp was visible nearly twenty-five miles out at sea. Now thousands of visitors each year visit the lighthouse; it is a vital piece of Great Lakes culture.

Travelers with a geological bent might be attracted to the glacial grooves on Kelleys Island in Lake Erie, where the retreating continental glaciers scoured a series of trenches, perhaps fifteen

And he wore cool cream pants, the Mayor of Gary, and white shoes, and a barber had fixed him up with a shampoo and a shave and he was easy and imperturbable though the government weather bureau thermometer said 96 and children were soaking their heads at bubbling fountains on the street corners.

Carl Sandburg
"The Mayor of Gary"

feet deep and a hundred feet long, into the rocks. Few other places on the continent show the grinding effects of the glaciers in such detail. Unfortunately, the state of Ohio has chosen to completely surround the grooves with a high cyclone fence. Photography is out of the question, and, indeed, squinting at a geological marvel through the links of a fence is enough to put one off the science for life.

Numerous though they are, public parks occupy only a small proportion of the Great Lakes shorelines, and the true shoreline buff will wish to wander farther afield. This wandering, however, presents a problem. The Great Lakes shoreline presents great variety, but one feature of the scene recurs with numbing monotony: the sign, variously phrased, warning the trespasser to keep out. Most of the anti-trespassers mania has been fostered by owners of residences, either permanent or seasonal, who crave privacy and are fearful of vandalism and theft. These natural instincts are difficult to quarrel with. But the morality of the private ownership of beach lands is open to question, particularly given the rate at which our wilderness is diminishing. In many of the coastal areas of the United States, lawsuits brought by public-interest organizations have established public rights to at least portions of beaches, usually the strip below the high-tide mark. On the Great Lakes, however, the tideline standard is meaningless. The lake tides are too small to be discernible, and their effects are masked by routine wave action. An appropriate standard in this case might be the vegetation line, for below this line the beach is actively washed, shaped, and influenced by the public's waters.

But public action on behalf of the Great Lakes shores has been minimal. Until such time as a doctrine of protection can be established, a major portion of the Great Lakes shorelines will be closed to visitors. And until a public clamor halts the construction of new residential areas directly on the shorelines, more and more choice places will be consigned to memory.

Every once in a while a striking exception to the keep-out syndrome crops up. One particularly satisfying exception exists on an exquisite beach on Manitoulin Island. There, one untenanted cottage in a group of three bears a sign on its door which reads: "This is private property. I keep it unlocked for your convenience. Please use it, but treat it as you would your own home as a favor to me." The unfurnished interior and the grounds of the cottage are spotless. Notes of thanks left by grateful folk who have taken shelter in the cottage are often found.

Perhaps surprisingly, long stretches of beach on the Great Lakes may still be found which are not publicly dedicated and are presumably privately owned but remain unfenced and unposted. Some of these shores are little forest hideaways on the Upper Lakes, but the bulk of the easily accessible unused shoreline lies in the agricultural areas bordering the Lower Lakes.

Most of the western shore of Lake Michigan, the western shore of Lake Huron, both shores of Lake Erie, and the northern shore of Lake Ontario consist of fields that stretch unbroken from a highway to the lake. To all appearances the fields end at the water, but typically a bank ten to twenty feet in height and a narrow beach separate them from the water. Hikers can scramble down the bank to the water at a road-end or other right-of-way, but they must do this with care, since the banks are very steep, usually made of slippery clay, and occasionally covered with loose rocks. Once at the waterline, the shoreline prowler can often walk for miles without hindrance or evidence of civilization.

These neglected shorelines of the Great Lakes may seem dull to those who never see them up close but only pass by them on the highway. But the charm of these lands and shorelines really lies in the fact that no one has thought highly enough of them to build a house on them, fence them off, or establish a park there. The wanderer can approach these lands with an unfettered sense of discovery, perhaps to find something interesting that has been overlooked by the rest of humanity, some new facet of the Great Lakes that can be hoarded as a private experience.

These shorelines are not beautiful by the standards of the Lakes. They have no high limestone or granite bluffs, no birch or evergreen forests pressing upon the beach, no sand dunes receding into the horizon. The water is usually murky due to runoff from the land. But they exist, available to anyone, and offer the opportunity for solitude, often just out of sight of the large Great Lakes cities. On the beach below the bank, the sights and most of the sounds of civilization are cut off, and a full range of small delights wait to enrich the life of a shoreline buff—not the least of which is the chance for a catnap in the warm sun followed by a plunge in the waves.

Unused land in these parts of the United States and Canada is disappearing quickly. Some of the better shoreline locations are being bought up by public agencies and turned into parks—a wise step in terms of preservation and accessibility but one that inevitably destroys the intimacy with the land that beach wanderers seek. But more often these unused lands are being developed and closed off. Sometimes this closure happens in large chunks: The agricultural coastal terraces of the Great Lakes have become favorite places for the construction of nuclear power plants, for example. The shorelines provide ample land and an abundant supply of water for the plants and close proximity to load centers. Elsewhere the vacant shorelines are disappearing bit by bit. Where once the view from the road swept over an uninterrupted expanse of green fields leading down to the water, in many places that clean line of separation is now serrated by a snaggle-toothed row of mobile homes or ranch houses perched upon the bank. Paths or steps cling to the banks in such developments and "No trespassing" signs abound.

Unused land is residual land that lies vacant only because no one has gotten to it yet; it is valued only in terms of its potential for development, not in terms of its unique character. A generation ago the same was true for wilderness, but now we seek to preserve wilderness for its own sake.

We are slowly discovering the positive values of pastoral coastal landscapes and of narrow, unused and unmanaged beach strips. Techniques of land-use planning and easement acquisition are gradually being developed to insure that the shorelines will continue to have esthetic appeal as well as practical utility. But achieving this heightened awareness is a slow process, to date far behind the rate of shoreline consumption.

The problems are not limited to the insensitivity of speculators and developers, however. Eleven thousand miles is a lot of shoreline, enough to provide something for everybody, from bearded wilderness freaks to pin-striped shipping executives. But some 35 million people live in the Great Lakes basin, and each person can lay an equal claim to less than two feet of that shoreline. Who gets how much, and where? Who makes the decisions, and how? These questions have been resolved implicitly in the past, with the kind of casualness that too often accompanies abundance. We can and must be sure that they will be posed far more sharply in the future.

Lakeshore Planning

Chicago was built beside a great lake not simply to provide drinking water and transportation but also because this immense inland body of water must have awed all those who first discovered it in the midst of great plains. . . . Simply stated, Lake Michigan offers us a great body of open water, a reservoir of fresh air to clean the city, superb climatic control and unparalleled recreational resources. To the individual it may be most important as a glimpse of blue water through green trees, the sight of great clouds building up over a flat horizon, the excitement of powerful waves, the sense of an immense vault of silence just beyond the shoreline.

FITTINGLY, a Chicago citizens' group, the Open Lands Project, made this observation on the relation of the city to its waterfront, for Chicago more than any other city on the Lakes—perhaps more than any other city on the continent—has worked hard over the years to keep its shoreline available to its citizenry. Efforts to preserve the lakefront began in 1836, when Chicago was still a village. In that year three canal commissioners marked off an area on their map and designated it "Public Ground—A Common to Remain Forever Open, Clear and Free of any Buildings, or other Obstruction Whatever." Today, after nearly a century and a half of civic squabble, political warfare, litigation, and compromise, that public ground is Grant Park—by no means clear and free of all buildings and obstructions whatever, but still the gracious and elegant focus of the city's civic pride.

Lincoln Park near the end of Fullerton Street is a fine place to see how Chicagoans use their lakefront. On a warm summer day, a steady stream of foot traffic converges on the park. Some people veer off toward the zoo and the conservatory, but most continue up over the low bridge that crosses Diversey Lagoon. On the top of the bridge there is generally an audience for whatever might be going on below on the lake: rowing races in the long, narrow walled lagoon; the hectic activity of motor boats heading out of Diversey Harbor; or simply a few fishermen with canepoles.

Passing beneath the roaring lanes of Lakeshore Drive, the strolling crowd reaches the beach. Some turn right toward a narrow walkway that borders the sand; others head for a long stretch of concrete terrace separating the water from the adjacent parkland. This is a beach too, though not in the conventional sense; it is actually a swimming wharf. Swimmers clamber over the crumbling concrete edge into water two to three feet deep, and flop back over the lip like seals when they are done, to towel down and stretch out. Basking on concrete hardly qualifies as the last word in sun-bathing comfort, but most come prepared with foam pad, large beach towel, or cushion—and some claim to prefer it to getting all gritty with sand.

On a fine day hundreds of people congregate on the beach and in the park above it, and this area holds but a tiny fraction of the activity along Chicago's Lake Michigan waterfront. Twenty-four of the city's thirty miles of shoreline lie within public parks. The Chicago Park District has estimated that around 20 million visits are paid each year to the beaches alone, and that figure does not include visits to playgrounds, promenades, boat harbors, fishing lagoons, or other lakeside attractions.

Besides serving as a recreation resource, Chicago's public lakefront serves the esthetic function of giving the city, or at least major portions of it, a feeling of space. The view of the lake from a downtown office building or hotel, the glimpse of green caught in an eastward glance down a street, the fresh smell of the air as it blows off the water—all are intangible benefits of the city's lakefront policy.

Mistakes have been made, but for all the errors made and lessons learned in retrospect, Chicago's lakefront today more closely resembles the dreams of conservationists than the ambitious projections of developers. It is the legacy of a century of lakefront visionaries who fought for and designed a public shoreline. One of the first was John Rauch, a physician, who in the mid-1860s persuaded the City Council to close down the city's northside cemetery—his main concern was to check the spread of epidemic diseases such as cholera and smallpox—and to establish a public park on the site. The park was named Lincoln Park after the recently murdered president.

Soon afterward, Frederick Law Olmstead designed a matching park system on the city's south side. The results were Jackson and Washington Parks, the two connected by the grassy Midway Plaisance and totaling over a thousand acres. Today Jackson Park's beaches, picnic areas, play-grounds, and ball fields are jammed throughout the summer, but enough wildness remains—in the

Am I asking too much? Of any Sunday-morning balloon-man's spring in Chicago, that it fill the wishes of all young men in landlocked bars a little, waiting for their lifelong lives to start?

Or raise the hopes of Sunday-morning sidestreet solitaries all over town, to let them drift slowly and low. . . toward that wonderful garden where all things are possible? To all those now merely waiting for rain or bread or love or peace with a pinch of the salt of magic in it that will last till the big dark falls.

Nelson Algren
The Last Carousel

A second sky spread at the city's feet. . . .

Howard Spencer Fiske
"An Ode to Lake Michigan"

middle of the crowded south side—for green herons to find nesting spots along the banks of one of the lagoons.

The hero of the city's central waterfront was merchandising magnate A. Montgomery Ward. Between 1890 and 1911 he filed several lawsuits to enforce the "forever open, clear and free" provision of the canal commissioners' grant. He prevailed: The area was cleaned up, certain old developments were removed, and new development was stopped. The result is Grant Park, with its gardens, fountains, and unobstructed shoreline.

In 1909 architect Daniel Burnham developed a plan for Chicago that emphasized the city's relationship to its lake. In Burnham's projection the whole waterfront, virtually from city line to city line, would be dedicated as parkland, and a series of islands would be built just offshore to add more park space and to provide protected waters for boat harbors. He envisioned the central lakeshore as a broad basin, sweeping symmetrically to a series of manmade promontories and islands. Burnham's plan was officially adopted by the city in 1919, after its architect's death, but was never completely carried out, and only one of the promontories and one of the islands were actually constructed. They form the southern edge of the Grant Park boat harbor.

The most recent heroes of the lakefront are the countless men and women who battled against a proposed jetport in the lake. In 1967 the city announced that it was considering building an international jetport on eight thousand acres of reclaimed land five miles east of the city's shoreline. That the city was more than considering the project soon became clear; the administration, headed by Mayor Richard Daley, had decided to proceed with it regardless of objections.

The objections came quickly and in force, for Chicagoans could not imagine a more egregious assault on their city's shoreline. Civic opinion on this issue attained a unanimity normally found in Chicago only in graveyards on election day. The city had to give.

On May 10, 1972, five years after the furor started, Mayor Daley held a press conference. "I am unequivocally opposed to building a third airport," he declaimed, as though it had been his position all along and the press should have known it. "I am unequivocally opposed to building an airport in the lake. I say it with sincerity. I love this city, and I love its people, and this administration would do nothing to deface its greatest asset—the lakefront."

In his own way, the mayor was echoing the words of Daniel Burnham, spoken more than half a century before:

The lakefront by right belongs to the people. It affords their one great unobstructed view, stretching away to the horizon, where water and clouds seem to meet. . . . Not a foot of its shores should be appropriated by individuals to the exclusion of the people. On the contrary, everything possible should be done to enhance its natural beauties, thus fitting it for the part it has to play in the life

Lake Michigan has always been one of our most treasured assets and we deeply cherish it. We have generally prevented industry from building along the Chicago shore and thereby preserved its value as a source of recreation for the people of Chicago. Virtually all of Chicago's 29 miles of shoreline are devoted to public use including some 30 bathing beaches and eight marinas.

Former Mayor Richard J. Daley

of the whole city. It should be made so alluring that it will become the fixed habit of the people to seek its restful presence at every opportunity.

In 1942 the City Council of Cleveland, Ohio, adopted a lakefront plan for its Lake Erie shoreline. Responding to the same needs and desires of the population that had motivated Daniel Burnham in Chicago, the plan set a goal of creating a nearly continuous strip of parkland from city limit to city limit. Industry would be largely confined to the lower Cuyahoga River. Now Clevelanders, too, would have green fields and promenades.

If Daniel Burnham were alive today he would doubtless be disappointed at how incompletely his plan has been implemented in Chicago. But an exploratory tour of the Cleveland waterfront quickly reveals that, if Chicago has allowed Burnham's plan to be compromised in places, Cleveland may as well have had no plan at all.

The difficulty, and a very considerable one, is finding Cleveland's waterfront in the first place. No benign scenic drive can mitigate the central problem of the freeways that slash through the city and in most places form an impenetrable wall blocking the lakefront. With cunning and patience it is possible to get over or under the freeways to the lake, but the effort is not noticeably well rewarded.

The city has two parks, one on each side of town. To the east, Gordon Park seems to get relatively little use, possibly because it offers so little for use. It is a small patch of green, walled off from the city by a freeway, to all appearances untended and unloved.

Edgewater Park, on the west side of the city, is more prepossessing in form and shows evidence of more use than Gordon Park, although it is even harder to find. But it is dead. The lawns are patchy, weeds erupt through the concrete walkways and structures, and the effects of vandalism have accumulated to the point where hardly an intact and unmarred object remains in the park. Litter is everywhere, and a sense of desolation and sadness pervades the entire area.

Gordon and Edgewater parks occupy only a small portion of the waterfront. With respect to public access, most of the rest is wasteland. The greater part of the city's lakefront is a narrow, unusable strip of land along the edge of the freeway. Near the mouth of the Cuyahoga, the shore is littered with vast junkyards and ancient light industries. One of the few modern structures to be found is the United States Post Office. Since the building is windowless and dockless, one wonders why it was built on such potentially prime lakefront land.

The dominant facility on Cleveland's downtown waterfront is Burke Airport. The people who use it are mainly those who can afford to own or charter private planes; it is primarily a general aviation field with very little commercial traffic. The saddest commentary on the airport is that it was built in the 1950s, well after the City Council agreed to dedicate the lakefront to public use.

The necessity for parks was so little appreciated during the early days of our city, that it is said a plat of ground of several acres in extent lying on the bank of the Lake was given to the then village of Cleveland for the purpose of a park, on the sole condition that the trustees should take measures to fence it in. Unfortunately there was not sufficient enterprise or liberality on the part of the trustees to appropriate a few dollars to carry out this condition; consequently, the land reverted to the donor.

Council Committee Report, 1865

In November, 1874, a loan for fifty thousand dollars was authorized, and the commissioners immediately began the improvements and pushed them forward with energy and discretion until was completed one of the largest, most unique and beautiful of all the parks of Cleveland. Covering ten and a half acres, and overlooking for nearly half a mile the grand expanse of Erie, [Lake View Park] is the constant resort of all classes of people. Its refreshing verdure and cool fountains lend a glad charm to the restless, busy lake.

W. Scott Robison, 1887

Clevelanders regularly visit one spot, and one spot only, in the city to take advantage of the Lake Erie shore—the same one they visited before the lakefront plan was adopted in 1942. At a public dock downtown, at the foot of Ninth Street, city residents mingle, look out at the lake, watch the waves crash against the concrete, and leave for "scenic" boat tours of the waterfront and the river.

Of course, the freeways, post office, airport, and all the rest were built for good reason along the lakefront even when the city's official policy was to reserve the shorelines for public parks. They were built there because the land was cheap, and the land was cheap because the waterfront had already been stripped of its value by decades of neglect. Generations of decision makers who failed to realize that a lakefront can be, to quote Richard Daley, a city's "greatest asset," were apparently unable to discern which commercial, industrial, and government-financed facilities truly needed waterfront locations and which would constitute bad use of prime property.

Cleveland's situation may be improving, however. In the mid-1970s, the City Council, realizing the absurdity of continuing to follow a plan that had been completely ignored for more than thirty years, voted to scrap the 1942 plan and ordered the City Planning Commission to draw up a new one. Cleveland can still provide itself with a front lawn to Lake Erie, and at least some people within the city government are working to do so. They may yet prove that no urban shoreline is irretrievably lost to urban decay—not even Cleveland's.

In the mid-1960s, Toronto suddenly and enthusiastically took note of its lakefront and decided to make something of it. The city examined the fifty-mile reach of shoreline in its urban embrace and concluded: "To not use this gift is wasteful. To spoil it is extravagant." This decision seems to have been a signal for all the city's overlapping governmental jurisdictions to get into the act of waterfront planning and development. Within a few years, projects were developed, buildings were constructed, and high-rises were proposed by public agencies and private concerns alike. Even the national government got involved; it bought up an 86-acre stretch of lakefront and announced that this area would be developed into Harbourfront Park, intended to open up Toronto's downtown lakefront to public use. Other plans involving increased housing, expansion of parklands, and improved port facilities were proposed. Toronto was seemingly trying to make up in five years for sixty years of lakefront neglect.

By 1972, it was clear that not enough thought had been given to how all these projects fit together, or what the ultimate mixture of shoreline facilities would be. Nor had transportation channels to and from the waterfront been properly worked out. Finally, waterfront plans had not been sufficiently coordinated with proposals for other nearby parts of the city.

To give focus to the chaotic energy motivating waterfront development, the Toronto City

Council established the Central Waterfront Planning Committee (CWPC). The planning undertaken by the CWPC is unusual in the extent to which public involvement was solicited. Through the press, meetings with civic groups, the publication of explanatory brochures, and other techniques, the planners convinced Toronto residents that the decisions affecting lakefront development were ultimately theirs. Public response was encouraging and useful. With respect to the national Harbourfront proposal, for instance, hundreds of diverse ideas emerged from groups and individual citizens. Among the suggested uses for this area were the following: "boardwalk, bicycle path, garden"; "year-round international casino"; "low-income housing"; "conversion of grain elevators into sewage plants or compost heaps"; "Linnean garden—a collection of near-extinct plants"; "high-performance power-boat regattas"; "railway boxcar restaurant"; "physical fitness center"; "farmers' market in old iron foundry"; "simulated rockface climbing wall"; "French festival of music and dance."

Whatever shape the lakefront ultimately assumes—if, indeed, it ever stops evolving—it has already served to reawaken Toronto residents' interest in their Lake Ontario shoreline. Toronto has committed itself to transforming its lakeshore for the public benefit. The fact that this effort is under way should excite not only Torontonians but should inspire other waterfront cities.

If the Great Lakes have a Maritime Province, it is Prince Edward County, Ontario, which hangs down into Lake Ontario just west of the entrance into the St. Lawrence River outlet. The Z-shaped Bay of Quinte almost completely divides the county from the rest of Ontario, and a canal dug through the narrow neck at the head of the bay has made the irregularly shaped peninsula an island.

People in some areas of the Great Lakes region may rely more heavily on the Lakes for their livelihood, but in few areas is the feeling of being surrounded by water as strong. A visitor traveling around the county is constantly aware of the proximity of the shoreline—either that of the serpentine Bay of Quinte or of the many arms of Lake Ontario itself that poke deeply into the land.

Prince Edward County is not spectacular country. It has limestone bluffs, but they are not imposing; it has fine sand beaches with dunes, but none have the grandeur of the beaches along Lake Michigan. The country's rolling topography is not particularly distinct from the terrain of Manitoulin Island or the coastal areas between the county and Toronto. The Bay of Quinte is very unusual because of its sinuosity, but it lacks the breathtaking beauty of Lake Superior or Georgian Bay. In short, no one feature of the county is truly outstanding, but the region is a very special place nevertheless. It achieves its specialness not from any of its parts but from the perfection with which the parts fit together.

A few discordant notes do exist in this basically harmonious environment. By far the most prominent is apparent to the visitor who crosses the bay on the *Quinte Loyalist*, the car ferry to the county from the mainland. Looming at the head of the reach is a massive cement plant, a bleak structure that squats upon the landscape it has emasculated and begrimed. Nothing else of the scale of this plant intrudes onto the county's landscape, and in fact the construction of this plant may have forced county residents to think more deeply about the values of their region in relation to industrial development.

In the early 1970s, the Ontario Hydro Electric Commission proposed that the scenic Long Reach of the Bay of Quinte be spanned by a 230-kilovolt transmission line suspended from red-and-white towers reaching three hundred feet into the air. The Long Reach, with its atmosphere of a fjord, is the most beautiful reach of the bay, and residents resisted the idea of its being violated by the towers and cables and by orange balloons to warn low-flying aircraft. They allied themselves with Toronto conservationists and protested the proposal, making good use of mass-media advertising. The campaign was successful, and Ontario Hydro agreed, under pressure, not to build the crossing.

For a long time the county managed to avoid being colonized—that is, usurped—by city tourists and summer residents. Toronto and the cities at the western end of Lake Ontario lie as close to Georgian Bay and the Lake Muskoka district as they do to Prince Edward County, so tourist-resort and summer-home development engulfed large portions of the once-pristine north woods instead of swamping the Bay of Quinte region. Prince Edward County was able to drift through the first three quarters of the twentieth century relying more on its own heritage than on any help or interference from the outside world.

But in the early 1970s signs of change appeared. The north country filled up, at least that portion that lies within weekend commuting distance of Toronto. The construction of a freeway along the north shore of the lake cut driving time to the county substantially. With the building of a

new bridge, called the Quinte Skyway, accessibility to the county increased markedly. Shoreline real estate prices increased 700 percent between the mid-sixties and the mid-seventies. The several provincial parks in the area attracted, and continue to attract, more and more visitors each year, and cottages and house trailers became increasingly prevalent across the landscape.

The colonization process has drastic effects on an area, a fact to which other "discovered" Great Lakes regions bear sad testimony. An excellent example of an area in which the process is virtually complete is Wisconsin's Door Peninsula, the ragged western bow of the Niagara Escarpment that separates Green Bay from Lake Michigan. This region was first discovered by city folks around the turn of the century. The first manifestations of the phenomenon were some simple cottages tucked back in the woods and a few fashionable resort centers with large estates and verandahed hotels. Then came the summer stock theater, the first artists' galleries, and the boaters. Next a summer music festival was instituted at the high school. Gift shops opened, closely followed by the "gifte shoppes." Finally, several state parks were developed, and the transformation of a remote rural area into a tourist haven was accomplished.

More horrifying examples of the results of colonization are visible in Wasaga Beach and much of the adjoining region of the south shore of Georgian Bay. The beach itself, a long sand spit separating the Nottawasaga River from the bay, now consists of an endless series of amusement facilities. With its slides, bumper-car rings, miniature golf courses, trampolines, and go-kart tracks, it looks like a graveyard for past fads. Commercial entrapments that are passé elsewhere can still exist here because the land itself has lost the power to attract. Visitors to the area find themselves stranded in a wasteland with nothing better to do than try to enjoy the concessions. On warm summer evenings people who are bored with their lives in the city, and bored within the tiny confines of the cabins they purchased in order to escape from the city, stream out from the ticky-tacky summer slums that stretch up and down the shore and descend upon the brightly lit area. Since they become quickly bored by the banal entertainments, new amusements must be continually offered up, ever more garish and unrelated to the qualities that caused the area to become a resort center in the first place. The old concessions meanwhile die a lingering, paint-peeling death.

Prince Edward County cannot be frozen at its present stage of development to protect it from this fate. Landscapes evolve; they are not museum pieces. But it need not become dominated and finally destroyed by tourism. A laissez-faire policy on the part of the government would no doubt result in the ruin of the county, but Canada's national and provincial governments are highly conscious of the need for planning in land use and development.

In the late 1960s and early 1970s, the Canadian and Ontario governments cooperated in an effort to preserve natural, historic, and cultural values along the extensive series of canals and waterways that connect Ottawa with Georgian Bay and Lake Huron. These canals and waterways were developed in the 1820s and 1830s to promote commerce and to protect waterway transport from interference by Canada's aggressive southern neighbor.

Included in that waterway route is the Bay of Quinte. The two governments realized the special importance of Prince Edward County, so instead of limiting their attention to a corridor along the waterway—the planning approach used along other segments of the canal and waterway system— the planning segment around the Bay of Quinte encompassed all of Prince Edward County and the adjacent shoreline areas to the north and east.

Planning was undertaken by a body known as CORTS, the Canada–Ontario Rideau–Trent– Severn Study Committee, which was based in Toronto. But planning was not imposed on the county from the outside: CORTS personnel lived in the planning area and consulted with local residents continuously. In this way the CORTS planners did what planners too often fail to do: They assured residents that the ultimate plan would be accepted only if it had a solid base of local support.

At the same time, however, the committee did not succumb to another common planning mistake, that of assuming that something can be given to everybody, or that everybody's values can be maximized. The planners, backed up by local residents, kept a firm perspective on what values should be enhanced through planning.

Within that framework the plan incorporated a great many specific measures. Shoreline zoning was used to protect 55 percent of the specified planning region's shorelines from development; the figure for the county itself, including land actually in public ownership, was significantly higher. The committee decided that roads would not be widened to enable more tourists to obtain a superficial glance at the area but rather that existing widths and alignments would be maintained, in order that the existing scenic balance would be preserved. Historical preservation was stressed but with the understanding that zones or districts, and not just the odd buildings of exceptional importance, would be protected. The planners also decided that pleasant but expensive anachronisms such as the free ferry were to be retained.

The CORTS plan did not attempt to stop all growth or change. It recognized that people would move into the area no matter what discouragements were placed in their way. Therefore the plan called for the encouragement of small industry development in the area and active prevention of the unpalatable alternatives—the construction of huge facilities such as the cement plant, an exclusive reliance on tourism, or economic stagnation and poverty. Basically the attitude reflected in the plan is that if a planned development fits within the identity of the county, encourage it; if it does not, stop it.

The formal wording of a plan is less important than its basic spirit, on which the follow-through depends. To those accustomed to the dusty fate of most creative planning efforts, the attitude of the CORTS personnel and the local county residents is immensely refreshing. It is inspired by a spirit of confidence and betrays none of the listless resignation about the future of a beloved area so commonly found elsewhere.

This contrast is demonstrated in a remark made by one 82-year-old resident of the county, who describes himself as "a Bay of Quinte Bullfrog:" "The great thing about living in the county is that I don't want to die. If I lived in the city I might not care very much any longer."

The Pollution of the Lake Waters

THE WATERS of the Great Lakes vary from the clearest and most pure—in northern Lake Superior, where the incoming waters flow cleanly over their rocky, uninhabited route toward the lake—to the murkiest, downright dirtiest waters that border the heavily industrialized areas. And as the lakeside environments change, so too does the quality of the waters. Some of this change is natural, resulting from the processes of erosion. But the most drastic changes that have occurred in the Great Lakes waters are manmade, and the most significant of these alterations has been the introduction of pollutants of various kinds.

The history of contamination in the Great Lakes does not differ essentially from the worldwide water-pollution situation. Over the years a vast array of substances and waste products has been poured into the water in the mistaken belief that the Lakes were large enough to dilute and assimilate nearly anything. Until recently, when public awareness of the effects of environmental pollution increased dramatically, the dumping of these materials was completely unregulated.

As a result of this unregulated dumping, two broad categories of pollutants exist in the Great Lakes. The first category consists of substances that are in themselves contaminants; that is, they are directly harmful to aquatic life and, in some cases, ultimately toxic to human beings. The substances found in the Lakes cover a tremendous range from, for example, human excrement resulting from inadequate sewage-treatment systems to certain chemical elements, particularly heavy metals such as mercury, which have been poured into the Lakes through industrial outfalls. Spilled oil falls into this category of toxic pollutants, as do new synthetic chemicals, such as pesticides, which enter the water from outfalls, land runoff, and fallout from the atmosphere.

The second broad category of pollutants consists of substances that are not in themselves toxic but that change the water chemistry of the Lakes, and hence the nature of biological productivity. Excessive amounts of nitrogen and phosphorus are the principal substances of concern in this category.

On the Great Lakes, the PCB story is the most grim—at least, the most grim so far detected—

and also the most illustrative of what happens when toxic materials are poured into a natural body of water. Polychlorinated biphenyls (PCBs) are a group of closely related industrial chemicals that have been manufactured in the United States since 1929 by the Monsanto Corporation, the only North American producer since production was begun. In varying forms, these chemicals have properties that make them useful as filling agents in electrical transformers and capacitors, as additives in hydraulic and lubricating oils, as components in paint, varnish, and sealants, and as coatings for certain kinds of paper. An estimated 1.5 billion pounds of PCBs have been manufactured in the United States alone. Additional producers of PCBs are found in eight other nations.

Though PCBs have been around for nearly fifty years, only in 1966 was their presence detected in natural bodies of water. By then, PCBs were probably already contained in the body fat of virtually every animal that treads, slithers, swims, or wings its way across the face of the earth, for PCBs have attained the same global ubiquity as DDT and other pesticides. They are everywhere and in everything throughout the planet's food webs.

In the Great Lakes, PCBs are generally found in concentrations lower than one part PCB to 10 billion parts water. This proportion might not seem alarming at first, but PCBs are subject to the phenomenon known as bioconcentration. Thus a PCB molecule does not pass out of an organism's system after it has been ingested but rather is permanently assimilated into the body fat. Therefore, far larger concentrations of PCBs are found in the body fat of water dwellers than are present in the ambient water. For example, a bluegill fish can bioconcentrate PCBs by a factor of over 70,000. That is, a concentration of one part PCB per 100 billion parts water, which is fairly representative of the open-water conditions in the Great Lakes, can become a concentration of seven parts PCB per 10 million parts body fat.

This process works its way up the food chain. The bluegill converts a 0.01 ppb (parts per billion) water concentration of PCBs into a 0.7 ppm (parts per million) level in its body fat. A predator that eats the bluegill will be feeding on an already enriched PCB diet, and the molecules of PCB will in turn be concentrated in a higher proportion in its own body fat and other organs. PCBs have been found in the brains and livers of herring gulls at a concentration of 2,600 ppm.

A large-scale research effort to examine the effects of PCBs did not get under way until a few years after 1966, when they were first detected as contaminants. It is still too early to know all the consequences of the universal presence of PCBs, but what is known is sobering. Tests with bottom-living organisms, minnows, and other aquatic life have shown that even minute quantities of PCBs, in concentrations similar to those found in the most impacted areas of the Great Lakes, can cause physiological damage and reproductive failure in these creatures. Mink fed a diet of coho salmon containing a PCB concentration of 10 ppm showed a 71 percent mortality rate, and even at 5 ppm they suffered complete reproductive failure. Similarly, poor hatching success in herring gull populations in the Great Lakes area has been linked to the very high PCB concentrations found in the bodies of these birds.

Scientists at the University of Wisconsin have experimented with rhesus monkeys, the standard test animals for attempting to extrapolate possible physiological effects on human beings. After a few months of being fed a diet containing 2.5 ppm of PCB, the monkeys lost hair, developed skin lesions, and were subject to metabolic disturbances. Prolonged consumption at higher concentrations, up to 25 ppm, caused weight loss, serious metabolic and urinary disorders, irregularity in menstrual cycles, difficulty in maintaining pregnancy, production of undersized and sickly offspring, and death.

The agencies responsible for monitoring the purity of our food—the Food and Drug Administration in the United States and Health and Welfare Canada—have, as a result of these and other experiments, imposed strict tolerance levels controlling the permissible level of PCBs in human food. These tolerance levels are so strict, as they must be in order to safeguard human health, that they have halted the sale of certain kinds of Great Lakes fish. The lake trout, for example, has always been the prime eating fish found in the Great Lakes, but it is a top predator and is therefore particularly high in PCBs. Smoked lake trout may still be purchased at fishing docks around Lake Michigan, but the fish are trucked in from Lake Superior; local fish are too highly contaminated with PCBs to be sold. And if, as is possible, continuing research on the medical hazards of PCBs forces the health agencies to lower the tolerance levels, even Lake Superior fish will be deemed unfit for human consumption.

Action has been taken to phase out the manufacture and sale of PCBs in the United States, but these contaminants are relatively indestructible substances, and the billions of pounds that have already been manufactured will circulate through the global environment even after new production is discontinued. The contaminants will continue to find their way into the Great Lakes and other bodies of water for years. And, even if totally effective treatment plants could prevent the contaminants from entering the water directly, the problem would still not be solved, since specialists now believe that over 50 percent of the PCBs entering the Great Lakes do so through atmospheric fallout, having gotten into the air by burning of paper and other materials.

PCBs do decompose chemically and eventually become harmless, but at present nobody knows how long that process takes. An optimistic guess is that PCBs will continue to be a serious problem in the Great Lakes for twenty years after new sources cease entering the environment.

Because of their toxicity and universal presence, PCBs are the most serious contaminant yet to be discovered in the Great Lakes. But similar histories could be outlined for DDT, mercury, asbestoslike particles, and other directly harmful pollutants, for each has had a serious effect on Great Lakes water quality, and each has been poured freely into the Lakes for years. The modern pollutants—synthetic chemicals such as DDT and the PCBs—have another point in common as well: Their inherent toxicity was not even discovered until after they had become so widespread in the aquatic environment that no short-term corrective action could be taken. Only in 1976 did the United States Congress take preliminary action toward requiring that newly invented chemicals be screened before large-scale production is approved, to determine whether serious environmental health damage might be associated with their manufacture and use.

These problems of contamination are not unique to the Great Lakes, but the Lakes have certain features that accentuate them. First, the Lakes are heavily relied upon as a source of drinking water and food. The contamination of the Lakes by PCBs may ultimately result in the elimination of the commercial fishing industry, which has been important ever since the area around the Lakes was first settled. The decline of this industry would in turn cut off a significant source of the nation's protein.

Also, once the Great Lakes are polluted, they tend to stay polluted for a very long time. When sources of pollution are eliminated, a river will regenerate itself in a relatively short period of time. If the incoming water is clean, most of the contamination is washed out to sea. But the Great Lakes are vast basins containing huge volumes of standing water. Therefore, only a small volume of clean water would enter the system to flush out the already polluted water of the Lakes, even if the sources of pollution were miraculously eliminated. Of the Great Lakes, only Lake Erie, with its relatively small volume, has a flushing rate that can be measured in a human lifetime; for new supplies of clean water to purge the Upper Lakes of their existing pollution load would take centuries.

Ironically, Lake Erie is the Great Lake most often given up as a lost cause, a "dead lake." But the situation could not be more fundamentally misstated, since overabundance of life is what causes Lake Erie to choke and sicken. Lake Erie is suffering most from a surfeit of the second broad category of pollutants—those contaminants that are not directly toxic but which change water chemistry and affect the ecosystem in and around the lake.

Unless it is disturbed by a major geological or climatic event, such as a glacial epoch, every lake goes through a similar process of evolution. A lake starts its life as a relatively pure body of water, typically created by the scooping actions of a glacier. Little life exists in the new lake, for the simple reason that little food exists within the water to support life. The aquatic environment is sterile, or nearly so, and hence the waters are pure and dead. A young lake in this stage is termed oligotrophic. The purest examples of oligotrophic lakes are high mountain ponds above timberline whose small rocky watersheds contain little soil or organic matter. However, the outstanding example of a large oligotrophic lake is Lake Superior. It is young, it lies within a relatively infertile watershed, and it has been unusually free from human interference. As a result, its clear waters support relatively little life.

As the ages pass, organic matter and essential nutrients find their way into the evolving lake.

The members of Moses Cleaveland's party who surveyed this territory in 1796, ate delicious broiled rattlesnake and found both commercial and esthetic delights in barter with the Indians, but worried about "the subtil, baneful wind" off Lake Erie, which led straight to death if breathed through the mouth.

Herbert Gold

In essence, the lake becomes fertilized. Most often the limiting factor as to how much life the now-enriched lake can support is the presence or absence of two essential nutrients, nitrogen and phosphorus, substances common in soil, animal wastes, and the effluents of human society. As more nutrients are added to the water, more life occurs. A denser concentration of various species of phytoplankton develops, aquatic plants thrive, and the variety and numbers of animal species that depend upon all of this vegetative matter increase. At a certain point in this process, the lake is no longer termed oligotrophic but is known as a mesotrophic lake.

As the process continues and both nutrient levels and aquatic life increase, the new abundance of plant and animal life causes the waters to become murky, and shallow areas become choked with algae and mats of aquatic weeds. As this mass of living matter dies, it decays, and the process of decay consumes oxygen from the water. Decay also releases nutrients back into circulation so that new generations of growth can take place. At this point, not only is the total amount of life increasing, but the forms of life are changing. Certain species require clear, well-oxygenated water; when this is no longer available, these species disappear, as do the species higher up on the food chain that feed on them. A lake in this stage has become eutrophic—well-nourished—the opposite of oligotrophic.

The final stages of a lake's existence come when eroded soils, dead vegetation, and other substances begin to fill the lake basin so that the water becomes increasingly shallow. Eventually it is no longer a lake at all, but a broad shallow marsh. Ultimately the marsh fills up, and what once was an oligotrophic lake is dry land.

Lake Erie's problem, in addition to the critical contamination problem it shares with the other Lakes, is that the natural process of eutrophication, which ordinarily spans millennia, has occurred very rapidly in its waters so that the effects of the process can be measured in years. This acceleration can be clearly seen in the amount of phosphorus in the lake's waters. Chemists believe phosphorus to be the most critical factor for sustaining the increase of life in the lake. From the recession of the continental glaciation until 1942, a period of several thousand years, the level of phosphorus in the western waters increased from zero to 14 micrograms per liter. From 1942 to 1967, a span of twenty-five years, that concentration nearly tripled, rising to 40 micrograms per liter. The measurements used to indicate the abundance of life have kept pace: Concentrations of algae near Cleveland increased from 100–200 cells per milliliter in 1927–30 to 1,300–2,400 cells per milliliter in the 1960s.

While the lake has shown an overall abundance of life, some areas have temporarily died. Vegetative decay in the deep waters of the lake leads to oxygen depletion, a condition termed anoxia, because oxygen is consumed faster than it can be replenished. Samplings in 1973 showed that 94 percent of the deep water in Lake Erie's central basin was significantly anoxic.

The combined effects of eutrophication have caused a profound shift in the forms of life found in Lake Erie. The lake's most prized food fish require deep cold waters with a plentiful supply of oxygen; thus they have disappeared or are disappearing.

Even the composition of the lake's algae has changed. In an earlier stage of eutrophication, the predominant species of algae were relatively unnoticeable forms such as diatoms; now the principal algae forms are the blue-greens, the types that cause noxious blooms.

Lake Erie's water-quality problems are not uniform. Underwater landforms divide the lake into three basins of unequal size. The western basin, bounded at the east by Point Pelee and the Erie Islands, is by far the most eutrophic. It is, however, very shallow, so more complete water circulation prevents the kinds of anoxic deep-water conditions found farther east. The central basin, bounded roughly by Point Pelee on the west and Long Point in the east, has severe oxygen-depletion problems in the deep waters but is considerably less eutrophic than the western basin. The water quality in the eastern basin is superior; it is so high, in fact, that this basin is still considered a meso-trophic, rather than an eutrophic, body of water.

Lake Erie is by no means irredeemable. Indeed, the answer to its problems, in theory at least, is simple. To halt and, ideally, reverse the process of eutrophication, the total amount of living matter in the lake must be diminished; to diminish this superabundance, the inflow of nutrients that support life must be greatly reduced. In practice, that means reducing the inflow of phosphorus.

Seventy percent of the lake's phosphorus enters the water through municipal and industrial waste-water outfalls, the vast majority coming from the former; the remaining 30 percent comes largely from land runoff. Of the municipal fraction, about 70 percent of the American loading, and 50 percent of the Canadian, is due to phosphates in detergents. In other words, about 40 percent of the total load of phosphorus causing the eutrophication of Lake Erie could be eliminated by the single step of removing all phosphates from detergents.

The technology for screening phosphates from municipal outfalls does exist. But even if all phosphates were banned from detergents, the efficiency of phosphorus-removal facilities would have to be notably improved and the amount of phosphorus entering the lake from sources other than sewer outfalls—such as in fertilizers and animal wastes from feedlots—would have to be drastically reduced. These actions would be expensive and politically difficult to accomplish, but they are not impossible. Simply put, Lake Erie can be saved. The nature and solution to the lake's problem have been clearly identified. All that is really required to save the lake is money.

The solution will take time, even if the necessary reduction of phosphorus inflow is accomplished relatively quickly. Phosphorus taken up by green plants when they are growing is released back into the water when the plants decay. Much of it settles into the bottom sediments; from the sediments, it can be resuspended into the water over time. But unlike the other Great Lakes, Lake Erie has a relatively short flushing time. If the incoming waters are cleaned up, enormous progress could no doubt be made in the course of one or two decades.

Lake Erie is not the only one of the Lakes suffering from accelerated eutrophication. Lake Ontario receives Lakes Erie's outflow, so it too has been seriously degraded over the course of the last few decades. Most seriously, the southern end of Lake Michigan is not flushed out by a large through-flow of water; it has no tributary streams of any consequence, and its water tends to circulate internally in the southern end of the lake. If the southern end of Lake Michigan becomes generally polluted, centuries of effort would be required to clean it up. An "ounce of prevention"—in the form of disallowing new sources of pollution—could hardly be better placed.

We now know enough to beware of the possibility of danger in any substance that does not occur naturally in the waters of the Great Lakes. But still the argument is made that the clean Lakes—Lake Superior and most of Lakes Michigan and Huron—are somehow cleaner than they need be, and that we should set an arbitrary standard down to which they can be degraded without public detriment.

We may have learned from experience, but we are still not very smart. Leaving aside the morality of intentionally degrading a genuine wonder of nature, we do not know enough about the cumulative effects of pollutants, whether contaminants or nutrients, to take even the slightest risk in their use. Both the United States and Canada have committed billions of dollars to making dirty water cleaner. The next step is to undertake a similar commitment to prevent the pollution of the clean water that remains to us.

A TYPICAL Lake Erie fishing boat might retrieve five eight-foot-wide nets a day. The nets are set for perch and yellow (walleye) pike, and a reasonably satisfying five-net catch might amount to, say, one large crate of perch and about 130 more valuable pike. A catch of this size is a far cry from the usual yield when Great Lakes fishing was in its prime. Mid-nineteenth-century descriptions of fishing at such places as Bruce Peninsula in Lake Huron today seem barely credible. In those days fishermen waited on shore until they spotted a large school, and then they sailed or rowed out to gather in as many fish as they could get in one sweep of a seine. The seine was drawn onto the shore, and the fish were scooped out. At times, four hundred barrels of fish were caught in one cast of the net, and removing them, cleaning them, salting them down, and casking them took up to three days.

That time of superabundance came to an end for a number of reasons. One major factor was

The Threatened Fisheries

the general degradation of habitat that has taken place throughout the Great Lakes. Pollution has had a large effect in reducing the numbers of certain fish species in Lake Erie; eutrophication in that lake has affected the large food species. And, though pollution has been more limited elsewhere, its effects on the fisheries have been significant. Siltation, dredge spoiling, land filling, and other physical changes to habitat have also been harmful.

Another factor in the decline of the fishery has been overfishing. In the past, commercial fishing was regulated little, if at all, and certain species were harvested virtually to the point of extinction. The tendency to overfish was exacerbated by a phenomenon known as year-class structure. The populations of most fish species are not evenly distributed in age but are instead subject to cyclical baby booms: Once such a cycle is established, it tends to be self-perpetuating, for as each baby-boom generation reaches sexual maturity, it creates a new baby-boom generation. Thus, in certain years, the fishing for a particular species was unusually good, and fishermen would believe that their bumper harvests indicated improving fishing conditions. They did not realize that the huge crops of mature fish were abnormal and that succeeding generations then growing to maturity were very much less populous. Overfishing during the good years ultimately caused the populations to crash.

The blue pike of Lake Erie, for example, was hit by both overharvesting and environmental degradation. As recently as the late 1930s, over 11 million pounds of blue pike were removed from Lake Erie each year, representing about 40 percent of the total commercial catch. Over the course of twenty years, this figure consistently declined until, in the late 1950s, the population crashed altogether. By 1965 the catch was negligible, and today the species is gone.

During the last thirty years, by far the greatest disturbance to the Great Lakes fishery has been caused by the introduction of exotic species of fish, that is, species not naturally found in the Great Lakes but introduced either intentionally or inadvertently by human beings. Many exotic species have adjusted well; they range from smelt, which are a popular food fish, to the gigantic goldfish of Lake Erie. But two species, the lamprey and the alewife, have caused great havoc.

The lamprey shares with its relative, the hagfish, the distinction of being the most primitive vertebrate left in the world. Shaped like an eel, and often mistakenly called the lamprey eel, it retains down its spine a simple cartilage rod—a structural predecessor to the segmented backbone—and instead of jaws it has a round, barbed, sucking mouth with which it attaches itself to the side of a large fish, rasps open a sore, and destroys the host fish by sucking it to death. In short, the lamprey is a thoroughly unlovable creature.

The alewife, by contrast, has nothing distinctive about it beyond its curious name. It is a small, nondescript member of the herring family, the sort of fish that receives little attention under normal circumstances.

Both the alewife and the lamprey are oceanic, saltwater creatures. How they immigrated into

Lake Ontario is not known; they may have come in naturally over the years and maintained themselves in small numbers. In any event, both species were recorded in Lake Ontario by the middle of the nineteenth century.

Prior to man's intervention, the Upper Lakes were barred to the interlopers, for Niagara Falls formed an impasse. With the opening of the Erie and Welland canals in the 1820s, however, the lamprey and the alewife were given access to new habitats. Their full impact was not felt for more than a century, but during that hundred years both species slowly extended their range over the entire Lakes system. The lamprey was the first to establish widespread notoriety.

That the lamprey prospered in the Lakes is not surprising, for it had entered one of the richest fisheries in the world—its opportunities for prey were unlimited, and no natural enemies acted to keep its numbers in check. Methodically the lamprey ravaged its favorite food sources, the large, firm-fleshed species such as whitefish and lake trout—species that also happened to be the most desirable fish for human consumption. By the 1930s, all of the Lakes had substantial lamprey populations. By the late 1940s and 1950s, the lampreys' numbers had exploded, and the Great Lakes commercial fishery was devastated.

The harvest statistics tell a grim story. The average catch of lake trout in Lake Michigan during the years 1940–44 was over 6.5 million pounds; by the late 1950s, the fish had been eliminated as a commercial species on that lake. In Lake Huron the whitefish catch dropped from 3.5 million pounds to one hundred thousand pounds during the decade from the late 1940s to the late 1950s. Figures from the other Lakes and for other high-quality species are similar, though less dramatic. The lamprey literally sucked the life out of the Great Lakes fishery.

The victory of the lamprey cleared the path for the alewife, for the lamprey's victims were precisely the large predator species that had kept down the alewife population. With few predators left to hinder them, the alewife population grew unchecked. The first alewife to be recorded in Lake Huron was spotted in 1951. Less than twenty years later, alewives comprised 99 percent of the pound net catch on the lake.

The alewife first impressed itself on the public during a massive die-off in the summer of 1967. Beaches were piled several feet deep with rotting alewife carcasses, and bulldozers fought a losing battle trying to pile them into trucks faster than they were washing up on shore. States of emergency existed in Chicago and other cities where the waves of dead and dying alewives threatened to clog city water-supply intakes. The phenomenon was never fully understood, and nothing like it has occurred since.

The die-off did not seriously affect the alewife's ability to thrive. Today the alewife is the dominant fish species in the Great Lakes, and rare is the beach that does not have at least a few fetid carcasses on it during the summer. The vast numbers of alewives have caused severe ecological

There is no need to review the danger signs we've all seen . . . the signs on beaches in many areas saying, "No swimming—Polluted." We all remember the recent nuisance of dead alewives, the unseemly sight of weeds and algae along the shore and the massive oil slicks of only last summer.

Former Mayor Richard J. Daley

disruption, since they have crowded out many more desirable species that compete with them at one time or another during the life cycle.

The results of these disruptions to the environment—pollution, habitat destruction, over-harvesting, and the disturbance of natural ecological balances—are visible all around the Lakes. Abandoned fish houses, junked fishing boats pulled up on beaches, and decaying docks are everywhere. The unemployment suffered by men whose families have known no other life but fishing for generations is a serious problem.

That any fishing at all is done on the Lakes today is due to the fact that the lamprey has one vulnerability: It is very finicky about the streams it will use for spawning. Researchers discovered that spawning lamprey congregated in relatively few streams. A number of control mechanisms were invented, including electrified weirs. Finally, in the early 1960s, a chemical was developed that was deadly to the immature lamprey—at a life stage during which it lives for several years burrowed in bottom sediments—but harmless to other organisms. A crash program ensued, with notable success. Though lampreys still exist in the Lakes, their numbers have been reduced so drastically that populations of large fish can once again survive.

With the easing of the lamprey crisis, managers of state and provincial fisheries turned their attention to breeding the depleted Great Lakes species in hatcheries to replenish the stocks. The devastation worked by the lamprey had been so complete that to allow nature to take its course without additional stocking would have meant a long wait for a healthy fishery. Also, a stocking program involving predator fish was necessary to reduce the uncontrolled alewife population.

Stocking programs using hatchery-raised native fish, such as lake trout and whitefish, were accelerated, but fisheries scientists were also looking around for a fish that would meet two other criteria. First, a faster maturing fish was desired to speed up the repopulation process. Second, fish managers, particularly those in Michigan, hoped to find a fish species that would establish for the first time a major recreational fishery in the Great Lakes.

In 1966 the state of Michigan first introduced the coho salmon into Lake Michigan. The coho, originally native to the Pacific coast, have adapted well. They grow to enormous sizes on the abundant rich diet of alewives. The coho, along with other salmon species, such as the chinook salmon and the steelhead, have now been stocked in all the Lakes by a variety of fish-management jurisdictions. Although these fish grow very well, their spawning has been limited, and artificial replenishment of the populations through stocking from hatcheries continues to be necessary.

When the Great Lakes commercial fishing industry, or what was left of it, saw real progress being made against the lamprey in the late 1960s, its members were quite naturally jubilant. That jubilation quickly soured, however, as the fishermen came to believe that the new and improved Great Lakes fishery would be managed exclusively for the benefit of sportfishermen. Traditionally, only limited sportfishing activity had occurred on the Lakes. During the smelt runs, the shores were often crowded with people dip-netting or seining, and bass fishing in the shallows had always been popular, but the offshore fishery was nearly exclusively used by the commercial operators.

The introduction of the coho salmon in Michigan in an attempt to open the Great Lakes to sportfishing was spectacularly successful. Today on the Great Lakes, most particularly on Lake Michigan, salmon fishing has become an important recreational activity. With respect to dollars-and-cents impact on local economies, sportfishing is now far more important along the Great Lakes than commercial fishing.

In theory, both should be able to coexist. The new exotic salmon species were stocked for sportfishermen, while traditional commercial fish, such as pike, lake trout, and whitefish, were introduced to reinvigorate the commercial industry. According to commercial fishermen, however, sportfishing interests have persuaded management agencies that the traditional commercial species should also be available for sport purposes; as evidence, they point to a series of ever-more-stringent state regulations controlling commercial fishing. These regulations are not designed to ensure that populations continue to increase, they argue, but rather to make sure that sportfishermen get an ever-larger slice of the pie.

In fact, competition with the sportfishing lobby, although detrimental to their interests, is only one of the many problems endangering the future of Great Lakes commercial fishing. The industry suffers from the same economic conditions that have plagued other specialized enterprises, such as small farming and shopkeeping. Commercial fishing has little appeal for young people who can make more money doing easier work with fewer risks in other fields. The price and salability of prime Great Lakes species fluctuate with changing consumer fashions. Even without the pressure of sportfishing competition, the supply of fish is uneven and uncertain.

But one factor above all that haunts every commercial fisherman's mind is the widespread contamination caused by PCBs and other pollutants. The increasing concern of health agencies as to the effects of the consumption of contaminated fish on human health may deprive fishermen of the right to sell the species of fish that are most profitable, making an already marginal operation absolutely untenable. The Great Lakes commercial fishermen might thus become the next victims in a food chain that is being contaminated out of existence.

Sport fishing is nearer the heart of the average man than is commercial fishing. Whether he sits on a harbor breakwater fishing for carp or goes out in a powerful boat with complicated equipment in search of trout or walleye, the sport fisherman engages in a personal adventure. Even when he comes back empty handed he has gained something. Perhaps the final sizzle of fish in a pan is the least important part of the sport.

James P. Barry
The Fate of the Lakes

Hawk's Island: A Cameo Portrait

ONE DAY shortly before the turn of the century, so the story goes, a young botanist named Henry Chandler Cowles happened to be looking out of his train window onto the Indiana portion of Lake Michigan's shoreline; he was on his way into Chicago from the East Coast. He saw various kinds of plants growing alongside each other in patterns that he had never seen before. Cowles left the train at Gary, hired a horse, and returned to the portion of shoreline he had seen to study the vegetation in more detail. His excitement lasted for forty years, and from it came the modern science of plant ecology.

Cowles' interest in the Indiana Dunes may not have been sparked quite as fortuitously as this story suggests, but over the years he worked in the dunes, woodlands, and bogs of the region to develop pioneering concepts of plant communities and succession. One of his haunts, now called Cowles Bog, was declared a registered natural landmark by the Department of the Interior in 1965, to commemorate the role Cowles played in developing the study of ecology.

In fact, all manner of scientists have interested themselves in the Indiana Dunes region over the course of the last eighty years, for it is one of the continent's living laboratories of nature. The geologists who pieced together the early history of the Great Lakes collected much of their evidence in this area by observing remnant shorelines that still exist as forested ridges.

The dunes themselves are classic examples of the collaboration of water and wind. Over the ages the prevailing winds and currents have unceasingly supplied the south end of Lake Michigan with sand eroded from the more northerly shores. After it is deposited on the beaches by the waves, this sand is blown back from the beach by the wind. When it hits an obstruction, such as a piece of driftwood, it develops into a mound. Soon the mound itself becomes an obstruction, captures more sand, and grows larger; a dune is born.

The landscape changes continually. The dunes move inland as sand from the windward side is blown over the crest and falls on the protected leeward side. In extreme cases a dune can travel at a rate of fifty feet a year. Meanwhile, on the lake side, a new foredune is formed, and it too may then march its way inland.

The most dramatic manifestations of the dunes' motion are the tree cemeteries. Forests die and then are buried as the dunes move inland. Years later, as the dunes continue to move, branches and trunks begin to emerge from the sand, and eventually a ghostly forest is entirely uncovered.

Some dunes, because of oddities of shape and exposure, remain bare and move for a very long time. Most, however, pause long enough for vegetation to take root in them. The spare and tolerant marram grass is one of the first plant species to establish itself, and its extensive root network begins to hold the dunes together. Once that happens, other grasses and, eventually, trees have the opportunity to survive. When a dune is covered with vegetation, it is termed stabilized; it no longer migrates. Once stabilized, the dunes undergo the process of vegetative succession. The pioneer plants—marram grass, bluestem, sand cherry, cottonwood, and others—give way to jack pine forests, which will yield in turn to oak forests. Ultimately, a climax forest of beech and sugar maple develops if conditions are suitable.

Naturally, the oldest dunes in Indiana are those which are farthest from the lake, and indeed the very oldest were formed during earlier stages of the lake's development, when the waters were sixty feet higher than the current lake level. Now, an observer walking inland from the beach for about two miles passes through every stage of the progression just described—from barren beach through sparse grass and pine and oak forest to, finally, the beech–maple climax forest. Adding to the natural complexity of the region are the pockets which form between dunes; these pockets are without drainage, so interspersed among the dunes are cattail marshes, ponds, quaking bogs, and swamps.

The completeness of this complex system gives the region its enormous natural scientific value. In addition, the Indiana Dunes region, because of quirks in glaciation-related features, climate, and topography, contains associations of plant species not commonly found in the Midwest. For example, prickly pear cactus from the Southwest may be found growing very close to northern jack pine and Arctic bearberry. Each of the plant communities in the progression forms a habitat for its own specialized bird and animal population.

Cowles and his contemporaries were in a sense the modern discoverers of the value of the Indiana Dunes. Algonkian peoples had lived in the region prior to the arrival of the Europeans, largely because of the easy portage connection between Lake Michigan and the Mississippi River via the Calumet River system. The first white settler, Joseph Bailly, arrived in 1822, but his plans for a prosperous and profitable Baillytown never materialized. The region was not well-suited for farming, so the dunes were largely ignored during the nineteenth century.

Chicago began to seep into the region in the early twentieth century, but summer-home development, which boomed elsewhere, somehow bypassed the dunes. Well-to-do Chicagoans preferred to colonize Wisconsin and northern Michigan; a large part of the limited development that took place in the dunes consisted of simple houses built by academics, intellectuals, and artists.

One of the Hyde Park artists who eventually found his way to the dunes was John Hawkinson. In 1950 Hawkinson was struggling as a commercial artist, after having put himself through night-time art school on the GI bill. He started rambling through the dunes, which he remembered from his childhood, in part to teach himself how to paint and in part simply to enjoy Chicago's backyard wilderness. An acquaintance offered to sell him two acres of land off Barking Dog Road to use as a base. Hawkinson accepted. The land cost four hundred dollars, three hundred of which were loaned to him by the seller.

Hawkinson could not have made a better investment to satisfy his needs. The area of the

Here were oaks partly clothed in red and brown, a flash of red in the top of the sumach, blueberries and blackberries in red and russet, touches of dogwood, gray aspen, red maple and shad, weird shapes of sour gum, and thousands of red tips of the swamp rose. But the most poetic of all— the foreground carpeted with delicate rose colored grasses, now made more vivid by the brilliant light of dawn, and amongst the grasses glistened millions of rosy diamonds, the first frost of the year.

Jens Jensen
The Dunes Dawn

Indiana Dunes in which his parcel was located consisted of about five thousand roadless, unmarred acres, by far the largest contiguous unspoiled section of the dunes country. The dunes themselves were higher, more extensive, and wilder than those anywhere else in the region.

To reach his land, Hawkinson had to hike in about a quarter of a mile from Barking Dog Road along a path that he and others believed to be the original Indian portage trail. The route was used during Hawkinson's time by people trekking into the cottages along the lakeshore; no roads went to these simple houses, and cottagers either hiked in past Hawkinson's cabin or walked along the beach from the nearest roadhead. Gear and provisions were often loaded onto rafts and pulled through the shallow water of Lake Michigan.

In time these cottagers, along with the permanent residents of the area, began to regard Hawkinson as their local Thoreau, as he tramped over the dunes or sat reflectively at the edge of his own little pond. Achieving solitude was not Hawkinson's only intent, however. In his youth he had been a Boy Scout, and as an adult he believed that the scouting program was the best opportunity city kids had to discover the outdoors. Almost as soon as he had bought his land, he started taking Scouts and groups of schoolchildren out to the dunes.

To accommodate the children and his other friends, Hawkinson built himself a small cabin for overnight use, gathering the lumber and skidding it to the land on a homemade sled during the winter. Once the cabin was built, he established what he termed "an open-door policy;" a key was kept in a hole in a tree, and he gladly encouraged friends, friends of friends, and indeed anyone who had heard of him to use the place.

Though plans for turning the dunes into a park surfaced now and then, they were never realized and, in 1950, when Hawkinson bought his land, the best of the area was still what might be termed "everyman's land:" vacant, unprotected, undeveloped, and wild. Some of it was owned in small parcels, but much of it had gradually been picked up over the years by real estate holding companies more interested in speculation than in instant development.

The speculators were waiting for industry to come to the Indiana Dunes. In addition to being a unique ecological phenomenon, the region was prime industrial land, and the industrial heritage around the Great Lakes was notably stronger than the tradition for environmental protection.

In 1905 Judge Elbert Gary, a minion of J. P. Morgan, bought land on Lake Michigan southeast of Chicago for his company, United States Steel, and founded Gary, Indiana, which was to become, after Pittsburgh, the town whose name was most associated with steel making in the United States. The land was in a perfect location for steel making. The ore from the fields of the northwest could be shipped down from Lake Superior by water and unloaded directly at the plant.

Nearly as important was Gary's access to land transportation. Because Chicago, the nation's second-largest metropolitan area, is located on the west side of Lake Michigan, all of its linkages

It has been decided to construct and put in operation a new plant to be located on the south shore of Lake Michigan in Calumet Township, Lake County, Indiana, and a large acreage of land has been purchased for that purpose.

Judge Elbert H. Gary
U.S. Steel Corporation
Annual Report

92

to the east—railroads, highways, transmission lines, and pipelines—must bend around the south end of the lake and run through or adjacent to the dunes country. This concentration of utility and transportation facilities within a narrow corridor was unique to the area in 1905, as it probably is today. Coal could be brought up to the steel mills by rail, and finished products could be shipped easily to anyplace in the nation. The southwest corner of Lake Michigan shortly became one of the major steel-producing centers of the world, with several large steel mills scattered along the shoreline from the south side of Chicago through Gary.

None of this development need have bothered John Hawkinson when he bought his land in 1950, for out in his dunes, he was free. True, he could see the smudges of Gary from the lakeshore, and he had to pass through the filth on his way to and from the region. But the contrast heightened his feeling of freedom and gave to his young initiates an even deeper sense of appreciation of the wilderness. They explored the area's waterways in kayaks, fashioned their own bows and arrows and practiced archery, and in winter they learned to ski down the smooth slopes of the dunes.

Sometime in 1952 or 1953, a land-holding company offered Hawkinson a thousand dollars for his land. He was not interested in selling, in spite of the 150 percent profit that the offer represented. He explained that he had never had any money and that he never felt the need for it. But he had fallen in love with the land; that he did need.

Others felt the same need, and in 1952 they created the Save the Dunes Council in an attempt to organize dunes partisans and resist the real estate company that was buying up the region on behalf of an as-yet-unknown client. Shortly, the client's identity, and its plans, became known. The Bethlehem Steel Company, the second-largest steel producer in the United States, intended to purchase the largest portion of the dunes, including Hawkinson's land, and build an enormous primary steel-production facility—that is, a mill that would receive ore and turn out finished steel. Meanwhile, a subsidiary of National Steel Company, Midwest Steel, wished to construct a finishing mill on a much smaller property west of that coveted by Bethlehem. And the United States Army Corps of Engineers hoped to build a general cargo harbor between the two parcels. The harbor plan anticipated the completion of the St. Lawrence Seaway Project in 1959. Local backers hoped that the new Port of Indiana would bring in ships from all over the world.

From the point of view of Indiana's economy, this package was extremely logical. The trend to which Elbert Gary had given impetus in 1905 would reach its culmination: The last large shore-line site in Indiana would be fully utilized for a steel mill. The Great Lakes were about to become the nation's Fourth Seacoast, and the state of Indiana was in for a piece of the action.

The Save the Dunes Council was horrified. "There are other places for steel mills and harbors," they argued. "There is only one Indiana Dunes." Throughout the mid-fifties, they attempted to dissuade the companies, the Corps, and state officials from carrying out their plans. Simultaneously

Some Don't Want Dunes in Indiana
(To The Tune of
"Back Home Again in Indiana")

Some don't want dunes in Indiana;
Some want steel mills spreading smog
Across the bathing beach, on top of trees,
And killing frogs in bogs!

Some ones get rich in Indiana,
While the people pay the bills!
Take a good last look upon the sunny
sand dunes,
For they soon may be leveled by steel mills!

Pat Walsh

First, we have a remarkable example of Dunes, a shifting, moving, living landscape; a natural phenomenon which in itself holds much scientific interest as well as beauty. We have, as a result of the Glaciers many hundreds of years ago, a rare collection of Southern Flora which was deposited here and which can be found no further North; and Northern Flora which was deposited here and which can be found no further South.

Senator Paul Douglas
Speech in Senate,
May 26, 1958

the Council attempted to develop a plan to save the dunes, even against the opposition of those parties. They urged that a park be created at Indiana Dunes under the auspices of the National Park Service.

Meanwhile, the companies' real estate agents continued to buy up land. Much of it was already owned by corporations involved in land speculation; those parcels were easy to obtain. Indeed, most of the cottages in this section of the dunes were on land leased from one of these companies; the leases were simply not renewed.

Money talked to other landowners. The initial offer to John Hawkinson quickly doubled to two thousand dollars and then increased to five thousand. The companies were aware that opposition to their plans was increasing, and they were willing to pay premium prices in order to obtain control of the land quickly. What followed was a classic battle of corporation versus citizenry, in which the companies can afford to wear down the resources of the citizens. Still, support for an Indiana National Park was strong, and the environmentalists managed to rally for a number of years.

In 1958, Senator Paul Douglas of Illinois introduced legislation to create an Indiana Dunes National Monument. The bill received the support of many congressional leaders, and it seemed to the Save the Dunes Council and the other supporting conservation groups that a milestone had been reached. In his speech to the Senate accompanying the introduction of the bill, Senator Douglas concluded: "With all humility I ask for your support of this Bill to create the Indiana Dunes National Monument. I ask it in the name of the people of Indiana to whom it should belong forever; the people of Illinois who depend upon it; the people of the United States who are growing ever more alert to their disappearing natural resources; and the people, the millions upon millions of people, who are yet to be born who cannot live and grow and be happy in a tight little world of factories, of smoke and noise and unrelieved pressure."

In 1962, four years after Senator Douglas introduced his bill, the possibility of the park receded. Almost all the landowners had sold out. Hawkinson by this time had been offered $25,000 and had turned it down flat, but his neighbors had not been able to hold out.

In spite of growing interest in the dunes, one cardinal fact outweighed the enthusiasm of the conservationists: The companies owned almost all the land. The directors of Bethlehem, not noticeably affected by Douglas's plea, decided to take advantage of that fact and put the issue to rest. They had not yet received the right to build, but they had the authority to destroy. They began to sell the sand.

Bethlehem sold the sand from the center of its choice tract, the heart of the National Monument proposal, to Northwestern University in Evanston. Ironically, for years, perhaps generations, biology students from Northwestern had trudged across these dunes to investigate their unique ecological system. Now their university was hauling the dunes back home. Beginning in 1962, millions of cubic yards of sand were scooped up, loaded into barges, and deposited as land fill at Northwestern's lakefront campus.

In the following year, the Kennedy administration resolved to cut through the Indiana Dunes controversy with a compromise proposal. An Indiana Dunes National Lakeshore would be created but not at the site Douglas had proposed. Bethlehem, Midwest, and the Army Corps would get the heart of the dunes, and the public would get a crazy-quilt pattern of the best of the remaining land in the region.

Almost everyone was happy with this solution except the Save the Dunes Council and Senator Douglas. But they could do little. The choice was either to accept the compromise and get a federally protected lakeshore—which, though inferior to the land to be sacrificed, still contained many fine dunes features—or to continue battling indefinitely and get nothing at all. Within a very few years, this compromise was carried out. In 1966 the bill finally passed, and the Indiana Dunes National Lakeshore became a reality of sorts, although it did not include the land that had originally inspired the concept.

John Hawkinson supported the establishment of the lakeshore and would willingly have sold his land to the National Park Service, but it was not included in the plan. By the time the bill passed, Hawkinson was the only remaining original landowner on the proposed Bethlehem site. The offers had climbed to forty-five thousand dollars. One day he received a phone call and was told to name his own price.

He still had no price. The company attempted to break his tenacity by making it difficult for him to get to his parcel. It received permission from the county to close Barking Dog Road, but Hawkinson went to court. The company backed down and did not attempt to deny him access. But access got complicated. Ultimately, in order to get to Hawk's Island, as his land had been dubbed, he had to pass through a gate guarded by an armed attendant. Furthermore, the company permitted only Hawkinson and people actually accompanying him to get through; friends who came out to visit were turned back. That practice ended the "open-door policy," and Hawkinson resented it greatly.

When neither money nor mild intimidation of this nature succeeded in moving Hawkinson, the company simply went ahead and built the plant anyway, designing it in such a way as to work around Hawk's Island.

Hawkinson still went out to the dunes with his Boy Scouts. One by one the features of the land that he and a generation of Scouts had loved disappeared. But he still had his two acres, plus a buffer of several acres that the company had left, because they knew that he would haul them into court if his land were physically affected by the construction.

Though not the same as the wilderness he had once known, a few acres was enough for wandering around in. Life remained to be studied in his little pond; skiing was still possible on a limited basis; so was archery. Except for the construction noise, the vibrations, and the dirt in the air, Hawkinson and the Scouts could still imagine themselves to be in the middle of their old wilderness, in the heart of the biological miracle that had so enraptured Henry Chandler Cowles.

Hawk's Island end came in 1970. Hawkinson's wife Lucy was diagnosed as having cancer, and the family had only one asset with which to try to meet medical bills—the land at the dunes. Hawkinson called the real estate agent, who over the course of fifteen years had made so many trips into town to persuade him to sell. Now the agent called back in half an hour to offer him thirty-five thousand dollars. Done. Hawk's Island was gone. Two years later, Lucy Hawkinson died.

Hawkinson still works with children who come and visit him at the rural farmhouse in southwestern Michigan where he now lives. His passion is still to inspire these children with love of the land. His objective in life has always been, as he puts it, "to touch kids to the land and bring them together."

One group of people whom he had touched to the land met at Hawk's Island in the spring of 1969, for a picnic, one of the last festive occasions to take place on the land. The affair had been cleared with Bethlehem in advance, so groups of families were able to carry their picnic baskets through the plant gate and past the armed guards.

Incongruously, a small group of hills rose above the parking lots, the stockpiles, and the cleared and flattened sandy plain. The picnickers headed toward the hills, under constant observation by the plant guards, and followed the path to the ridges. From the crest they could look back over their shoulders at the Bethlehem plant and the Port of Indiana taking shape beyond it. Beyond that, they could see the smaller buildings of the Midwest Steel facility. Looking forward, they could see a little pond next to a lean-to cabin.

All day the picnickers reminisced, trying to recall old landmarks that had been wiped out. The children wrote Haiku verses and took them over to Hawkinson, who sat on the ground leaning back against a tree.

One little girl wrote:

> There is no safety in the woods;
> Footsteps of men are among the trees.

A power-house
in the shape of
a red brick chair
90 feet high

on the seat of which
sit the figures
of two metal
stacks—aluminum—

commanding an area
of squalid shacks
side by side—
from one of which

buff smoke
streams while under
a grey sky
the other remains
passive today—

William Carlos Williams
"Classic Scene"

THE STORY of Hawk's Island is a cameo portrait of today's Great Lakes. The days when anyone could get whatever he or she wanted from the Great Lakes region are gone, and every major proposal for the use of the waters or the shorelines conflicts with some other notion of how the resource should be used. For example, the number of high-quality food fish in the Lakes is finite, and the amount of money available for stocking is limited. Who should get the fish, the sportfishermen or the commercial operators? A small but precious amount of undeveloped shoreline remains. How should it be used—as power-plant sites in a society that is simultaneously energy glutted and energy starved, as home sites for the affluent, as parks, as industrial facilities, or as protected wilderness? And what about the water quality of the Lakes? Are we willing to pay the price to meet the standards that we set?

In the mid-sixties, an observer interested in diversity on the Great Lakes and in the preservation of public values would have come to a despairing conclusion when asked about the future of the Great Lakes. But not all the conflicts have ended the way the battle of Hawk's Island ended, and the decade from the mid-sixties to the mid-seventies has seen a number of encouraging new efforts. Ontario's reconstruction of Fort William, Toronto's rediscovery of its waterfront, the land-use planning developed for Prince Edward County and the Bay of Quinte region—all these developments reflect a new and enduring consciousness of environmental values. In the United States, four new national lakeshores were established between 1964 and 1976, and the concept of wilderness gained new legitimacy. In 1976 the United States Congress finally declared Isle Royale a wilderness. The same decade has also seen the continued use of phosphate detergents, the irresponsible development of lakeshore real estate, and the construction on the shoreline of more than half a dozen nuclear power plants.

The year 1972 brought two pioneering initiatives, each of which, five years later, remains largely unrealized. The first was the Great Lakes Water Quality Agreement, signed by Prime Minister Pierre Trudeau and President Richard Nixon on April 15, 1972. It states Canadian and American intentions to eliminate the discharge of pollutants into the Great Lakes in quantities that can be harmful, establishes a mechanism for determining specific water-quality objectives and standards, and declares absolutely that the clean Lakes will remain clean. It authorizes new studies to determine what additional actions may be needed in the future and charges the International Joint Commission, a body established by treaty in 1909, to administer the agreement.

As bold as it may sound, the Great Lakes Water Quality Agreement was basically an exercise in showmanship; it is not a piece of legislation and is thus not enforceable. The real future of water quality in the Great Lakes will be determined by the amount of money appropriated by each nation for the building of treatment plants and the vigor with which each nation sets and enforces stringent pollution-control standards with respect to private polluters. This point was brought home and

Saving the Lives of the Great Lakes

caused great bitterness when, in the year following the signing of the agreement, Nixon impounded billions of dollars in sewage-treatment funds appropriated by Congress, a significant proportion of which would have been spent around the Great Lakes. President Gerald Ford later restored the funds.

Still, though the agreement was basically an act of showmanship, much good has come from it. Under the auspices of the International Joint Commission, pollution experts from both nations have worked together to establish standards for every pollutant; though these standards are also unenforceable, they are a necessary step in establishing discharge limitations. Also, the agreement provides government officials and legislators with considerable moral leverage when arguing for stronger controls or more money. Finally, the new research sponsored under the terms of the agreement, along with the publicity that has accompanied this entire process, has made area residents far more aware of the nature of the pollution problems and more insistent, as well as hopeful, that something will be done.

Some progress has been made. Most of the tributaries entering Lake Erie are far cleaner than they were in 1970, a fact which is not only beneficial to those waterways but is also the first precondition for cleaning up the lake. In fact, some signs suggest that Lake Erie may be stabilizing, though experts are very cautious and warn that year-to-year variations in weather, water levels, and other conditions can mask general trends.

The second encouraging development in 1972 was the passage by Congress of the Coastal Zone Management Act, which recognizes that the coastal zone, specifically including that along the Great Lakes, has unique values and functions. The act is to be implemented by the individual states based on land-use plans which they are to prepare for their own shorelines. Each state took several years to develop a planning effort in response to passage of the Coastal Zone Management Act, but now each Great Lakes state has activity under way. The act does not guarantee the preservation of anything; in fact, a state could decide to reserve its entire shoreline for the building of nuclear power plants. One element of the act helps to make such an outcome unlikely, however. Each state is required to encourage public participation in making plans for the shoreline and to include public opinion in its decisions to the extent possible. Public participation is hard to define and harder to implement. But a strong, previously inarticulate interest in the Great Lakes shoreline has emerged, and that interest favors environmental protection over the trends of development that have prevailed in the last few decades. In Wisconsin, for example, the Coastal Zone Management program polled citizens on what values they wished to see enhanced on the Great Lakes shorelines. Well over 90 percent stressed that the natural and scenic features of the state's shoreline should be preserved.

But a plan for land use is only as useful as its backers are strong. Planning in itself holds no promise for the protection of public values on the Great Lakes, unless those who believe in the importance of the public values are at least as politically powerful as those who see the Lakes purely as a means of generating profits. Still, the Coastal Zone Management Act has demonstrated that the planning process can in fact generate political support for public values. It can stimulate discussion, draw out opinions that might not otherwise be expressed, and provide a framework within which citizen involvement can be focused.

In short, far-sighted planning that encourages public participation can help to develop a constituency for the Great Lakes. The lack of a large, well-informed, and active constituency up to now, even among environmental groups, has been a major factor in the destruction of the Great Lakes environment. Too few people cared enough to fight. Among environmentalists, the Great Lakes were traditionally the great issue that would be attacked as soon as some other, more manageable brushfire was extinguished. The public at large, having no access to the tools of combat, watched resignedly as the Lakes became dirtier and the shorelines more private.

Where resistance has been made—in such gallant efforts as those of the Save the Dunes Council—the localized nature of the endeavor has most often doomed the effort. While many local groups fight local battles, the groups and battles have not coalesced into a widespread campaign. In addition, too few people have drawn attention to wider relationships. The Bethlehem Steel plant at the Indiana Dunes, the cement plant in the Bay of Quinte, and most other Great Lakes industrial complexes all have in common not only the blight and pollution they have imposed upon their respective regions, but also the fact that none would have been built were it not for the existence of a highly subsidized Great Lakes shipping industry. Fighting for each individual site is not sufficient; just as necessary is an examination of the factors that lie behind, and cause, the specific conflicts.

As yet, no public-interest constituency comparable to those concerned with the Sierra Nevada or Alaska has developed around the Great Lakes issue, but the trend of activity is encouraging. Even such tentative gestures as the Water Quality Agreement and the Coastal Zone Management Act would not have been made in the first place had the climate of public opinion not been changing. Their existence, in turn, lends momentum to the upswing of public attention. The list of citizen's organizations that have been formed since 1970 to examine and work on various aspects of the Great Lakes is a long one, as is the list of previously existing organizations that are paying ever more attention to the Lakes.

The agenda to be worked upon is enormously lengthy but not impossibly so. Every effort must be made to accelerate clean-up measures and to make sure that no new major sources of pollution are introduced into the system. Innovative planning techniques combined with the purchase of easements should be developed and applied to keep residential sprawl from dominating the shorelines. To the extent possible, legal doctrines of public use should be explored and used to open up beaches even where shoreline development exists at the present time. More aggressive

efforts should be made at every level of government to purchase areas of exceptional quality and preserve them as parks, and established parks should be managed more sensitively.

Even more challenging, perhaps, is the need to establish the relationship between shoreline uses and water activities and quality. If, for example, maintaining the high quality of Lake Superior is a true priority, then new development in the watershed must be very tightly controlled. Similarly, the expansion of subsidized shipping must be examined closely, with an eye toward the impacts the shipping industry has on the Lakes.

More than 35 million people live in the Great Lakes basin, and the Lakes are expected to provide drinking water, beaches, jobs, fish, transportation, industrial sites, scenic views, breathing space, wilderness, and homesites for all of them. Besides the demands of the local population, the Lakes must meet the demands of two nations for everything from wilderness recreation to increases in the gross national product. Under these pressures, it is surprising that the Great Lakes have held up as well as they have. Although they have been greatly abused, they remain treasures of which two nations can be proud.

THE JOURNEYS

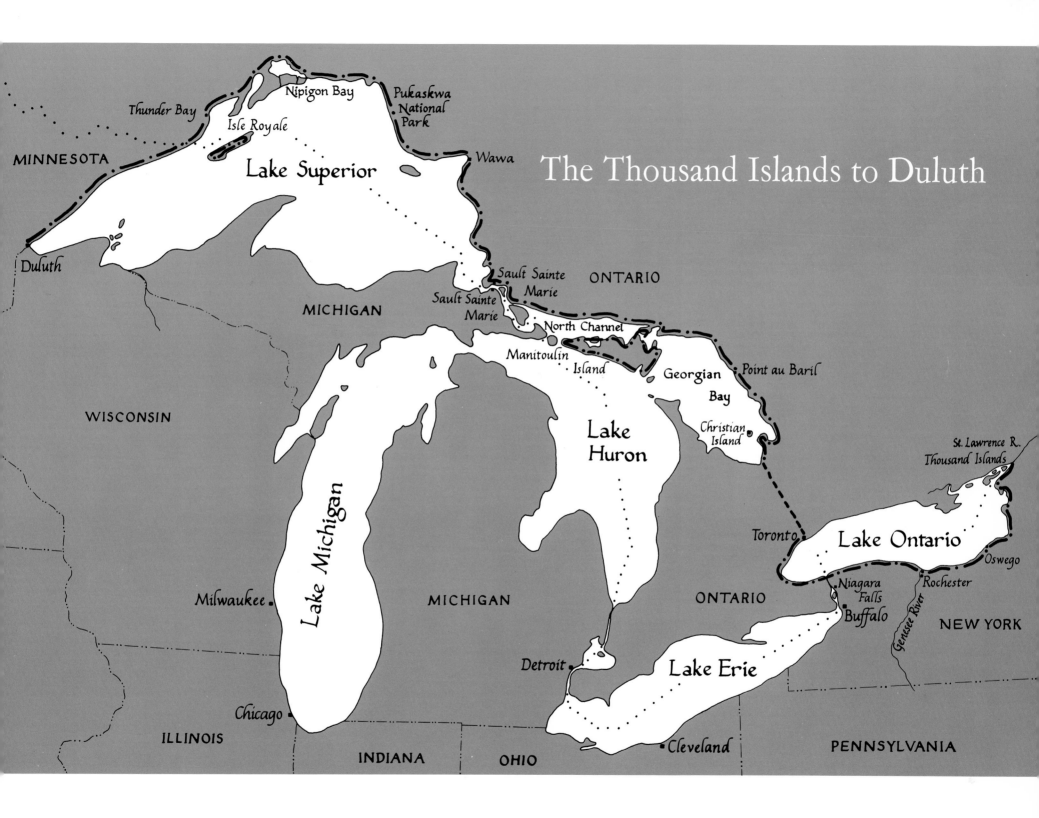

The Thousand Islands to Duluth

MINNESOTA

Thunder Bay

Nipigon Bay

Pukaskwa
National
Park

Isle Royale

Lake Superior

Wawa

Duluth

MICHIGAN

Sault Sainte
Marie

ONTARIO

Sault Sainte
Marie

North Channel

Manitoulin
Island

Georgian
Bay

Point au Baril

WISCONSIN

Lake
Huron

Christian
Island

St. Lawrence R.
Thousand Islands

Lake Michigan

Toronto

Lake Ontario

Oswego

Milwaukee

MICHIGAN

ONTARIO

Niagara
Falls

Rochester

Genesee River

NEW YORK

Buffalo

Detroit

Lake Erie

Chicago

ILLINOIS

INDIANA

OHIO

Cleveland

PENNSYLVANIA

Facing page:
On the American coast of Lake Ontario,
where it flows into the St. Lawrence River

Lake Ontario, near Oswego, New York

Near Oswego, New York

Chimney Bluffs, near Sodus Point

Near Olcott, New York,
between Rochester and Niagara Falls

King Island, Georgian Bay, Ontario

On King Island

On the Bruce Peninsula, Ontario

Left: Railroad bridge over the Genesee River gorge

Facing and successive pages:

Waterfall, Genesee River

River village,
upstate New York

Outer Georgian Bay

Gore Bay, Manitoulin Island

Facing page: Georgian Bay, off Pointe au Baril

Near Massey, Ontario

Facing page: One of many rivers that drain
the Laurentian Shield into Lake Superior

The Ojibways of Christian Island, Ontario, in Georgian Bay

Elder of the Ojibway

Ojibway charcoal worker

On the Council House steps

The old lighthouse at Pointe au Baril

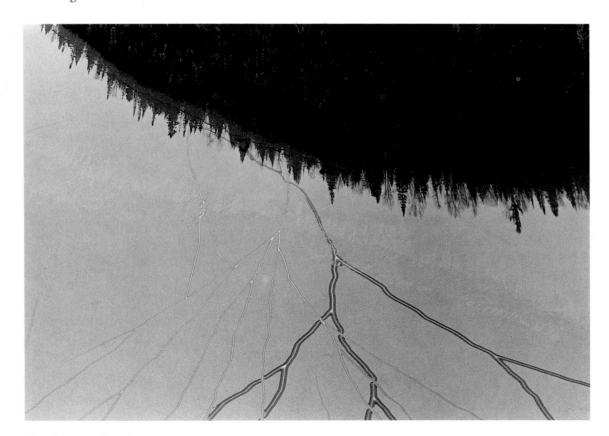

Near Massey, Ontario

The North Channel of Lake Huron, between Manitoulin and the Ontario mainland

Barge caught in ice on the St. Marys River,
on the way to Sault Sainte Marie

In the Soo Locks at Sault Sainte Marie;
Michigan side in foreground, Canada across the river

Steel plant at Sault Sainte Marie

130

Facing page: Old Woman Bay, near Wawa, Ontario

North shore, Lake Superior

Near Duluth

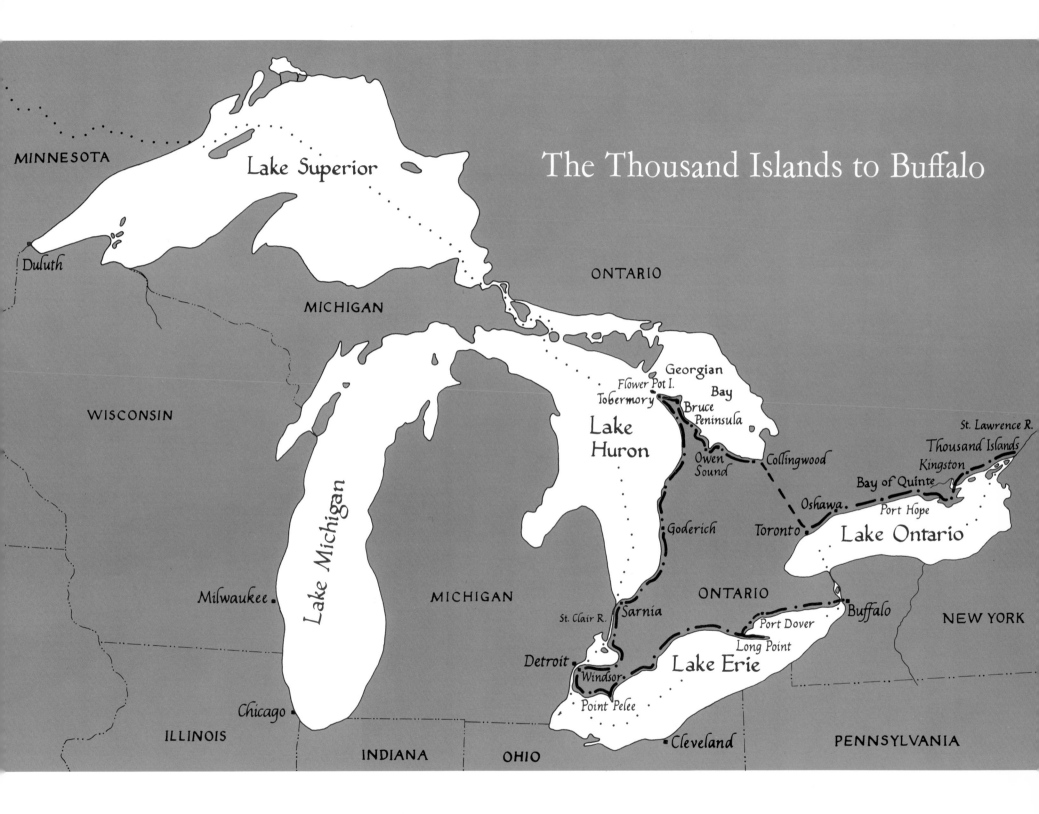

The Thousand Islands to Buffalo

MINNESOTA

Duluth

Lake Superior

MICHIGAN

WISCONSIN

ONTARIO

Lake Michigan

Georgian
Bay

Flower Pot I.

Tobermory

Bruce
Peninsula

Lake
Huron

Owen
Sound

Collingwood

St. Lawrence R.

Thousand Islands

Kingston

Bay of Quinte

Oshawa

Port Hope

Lake Ontario

Toronto

Goderich

Milwaukee

MICHIGAN

ONTARIO

St. Clair R.

Sarnia

Detroit

Windsor

Port Dover

Long Point

Buffalo

NEW YORK

Lake Erie

Chicago

Point Pelee

ILLINOIS

INDIANA

OHIO

Cleveland

PENNSYLVANIA

Canadian shore of Lake Ontario,
near the entrance to the St. Lawrence

Near Port Hope, Ontario

Facing page: The Thousand Islands

Between Port Hope and Oshawa

In Thousand Islands Park, near Alexandria Bay

Facing page: In Kingston Harbor

Near Collingwood, Ontario

Lion's Head, Bruce Peninsula

On Lake Huron

Upper Georgian Bay region: the transition stage, called "muskeg," of water becoming land

Interior of fishing boat, near Port Dover, Ontario

Facing page: Northwestern coast of the Bruce Peninsula

The Scarborough Bluffs, near Toronto

Facing page: The Bruce Peninsula

Flower Pot Island
Facing page: Toronto, January, 1976

Looking across the St. Clair River from Sarnia to Port Huron

On the Detroit River, near Windsor

Between Sarnia and Windsor

Niagara Falls to Chicago

MINNESOTA

Lake Superior

Duluth

ONTARIO

MICHIGAN

WISCONSIN

Straits of Mackinac

Beaver
Island

Mackinaw City

Georgian
Bay

Sleeping
Bear Dunes

Alpena

Lake
Huron

Traverse City

Saginaw Bay

Lake Michigan

Bay City

Toronto

Lake Ontario

Muskegon

Niagara Falls

Milwaukee

MICHIGAN

Port Huron

ONTARIO

Buffalo

NEW YORK

Lake St.
Clair

Detroit

Lake Erie

Chicago

Indiana
Dunes

Erie

ILLINOIS

Michigan City

Cleveland

Gary

Toledo

PENNSYLVANIA

INDIANA

OHIO

Sandusky

155

In the gorge below Niagara Falls

Facing page: Niagara Falls in winter

Boathouses,
Sandusky

Creeping dune, Indiana Dunes

Facing page:
Industry on the Michigan coast
of Lake Huron

On a tributary of the Niagara, near Lackawanna, New York

Erie, Pennsylvania

In the neighborhood of Lake St. Clair, near Detroit

Near Harbor Beach, Michigan

Sucker-fishing on Lake Huron

In the Straits of Mackinac, near Mackinaw City

Rough ice in the Straits of Mackinac

Near Cross Village, Michigan

Near Traverse City, Michigan

On the Leelanau Peninsula, above Sleeping Bear Dunes

Sleeping Bear Dunes

Near Gary, Indiana

Near Michigan City, Indiana

Chicago to Duluth

MINNESOTA

Lake Superior

Copper Harbor
Hancock
Keweenaw
Peninsula

Apostle
Islands

Whitefish
Point

Duluth

Pictured
Rocks

Sault Sainte
Marie

ONTARIO

Ashland

Marquette

Munising

Sault Sainte
Marie

Montreal R.

MICHIGAN

Manistique

De Tour

Straits of Mackinac

Escanaba

Georgian
Bay

WISCONSIN

Menominee

Green Bay

Door
Peninsula

Lake
Huron

Sturgeon
Bay

Lake Michigan

Toronto

Lake Ontario

MICHIGAN

ONTARIO

Milwaukee

Buffalo

Detroit

NEW YORK

Chicago

Cleveland

Lake Erie

ILLINOIS

INDIANA

OHIO

PENNSYLVANIA

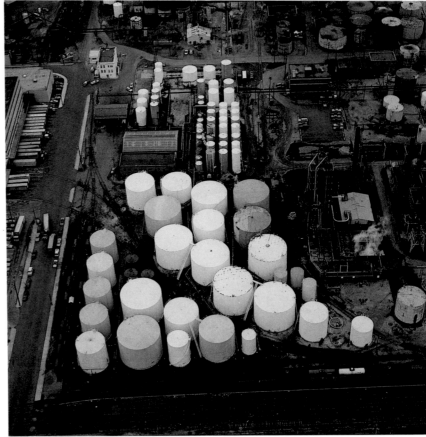

Outside Chicago

Chicago from the lake

Heading into Chicago's harbor

Duck boat, just up the coast from Chicago

Fishing boat on the Lake Michigan shore,
near the Indiana-Wisconsin border

On Wisconsin's Door Peninsula, above Sturgeon Bay

Near Tahquamenon Falls, Michigan

Facing page: Mackinac Bridge, joining the
upper and lower peninsulas of Michigan

Marsh, near Munising, Michigan   *Facing page:* Ice floes, Whitefish Point
Overleaf: "Miner's Castle" and the Pictured Rocks National Lakeshore

At the mouth of the Montreal River, which forms the
Michigan-Wisconsin border at Lake Superior
Facing page: Near Ashland, Wisconsin

Mackinac Island

Facing page: Madeline Island,
the largest of the Apostle Islands

Near Whitefish Point, Michigan

Sault Sainte Marie, American side

Grand Sable Dunes, east of the Pictured Rocks

Duluth

Duluth

THE FACES OF THE GREAT LAKES

was designed by Klaus Gemming, New Haven, Connecticut,
and printed in four-color and fine-screen duotone process
by George Rice and Sons, Los Angeles, California,
on 80-lb. Consolidated Centura Dull coated paper.
The text and display lines were set in Monotype Garamond.
The book was bound in Holliston Roxite Linen
by Lincoln & Allen Company, Portland, Oregon.
The maps were drawn by Gay Walker, Madison, Connecticut.

SIERRA CLUB BOOKS